the essential marketing sourcebook

Second edition

ROS JAY

FINANCIAL TIMES
PITMAN PUBLISHING

D0582862

FINANCIAL TIMES MANAGEMENT
128 Long Acre, London WC2E 9AN
Tel: +44 (0)171 447 2000
Fax: +44 (0)171 240 5771
Website: www.ftmanagement.com

A Division of Financial Times Professional Limited

First published in Great Britain 1996
Second edition 1998

© Financial Times Professional Limited 1998

The right of Ros Jay to be identified as author of this
work has been asserted by her in accordance with the
Copyright, Designs and Patents Act 1988.

British Library Cataloguing in Publication Data
A CIP catalogue record for this book can be obtained from the British Library.

ISBN 0 273 63108 X

This publication is designed to provide accurate and authoritative information in
regard to the subject matter covered. The publisher and contributors make no
representation or warranty, express or implied, with regard to the accuracy of the
information contained in this book and cannot accept any responsibility or liability
for any errors or omissions that it may contain. Further, no responsibility for loss
occasioned to any person acting or refraining from acting as a result of the material
contained in this publication will be accepted by the publisher or contributors.

10 9 8 7 6 5 4 3 2 1

Typeset by Pantek Arts, Maidstone, Kent
Printed and bound in Great Britain by Bell and Bain Ltd, Glasgow

The Publishers' policy is to use paper manufactured from sustainable forests.

SURVEYS AND REPORTS, 1998

The following surveys, reports and publications are produced by the organisations which have contributed to this book. You will find listed many of the full reports from which we have reproduced extracts in this book, along with other relevant publications. If you would like to order any of the surveys, reports or other publications listed here, the full contact details of the organisations are in Appendix II on page 303. Prices may not include extras such as VAT, and postage and packing.

Planning and preparation

Planning To Keep One Step Ahead, Barclays Bank plc Small Business Services, September 1996, free

Marketing and The Small Firm, Barclays Bank plc Small Business Services, May 1997, free

Manufacturing – the Marketing Solution, Chartered Institute of Marketing, 1995, £105

ESOMAR Prices Study 1994, ESOMAR, 1995, free

Using Market Research to Grow Your Business, Institute of Management, Sept. 1994, £15.99

The Survey Guide, The Survey Shop, Nov. 1995, free

Survey on the Editorial Use of Surveys, The Survey Shop, Dec. 1995, free

Direct marketing

Practitioners' Guide to Direct Marketing, to be published Spring 1998

Dataculture, The Henley Centre for Forecasting Ltd, 1997

DMIS Sector Intelligence Reports, Direct Mail Information Service, 1997

First Impressions Count, Marcus Child, Director of Training at Managing the Service Business (MSB) Ltd, 1997

Business Databases – A Study of External Lists and In-House Database Usage, Direct Mail Information Service, 1997

Direct Mail Trends Survey, Direct Mail Information Service, 1995

Commonsense Direct Marketing, The Drayton Bird Partnership, 3rd edition 1994, £27.50

How to Write Sales Letters that Sell, The Drayton Bird Partnership, Nov. 1994, £25.

Direct Mail Trends Survey 1994, Direct Mail Information Service, 1994, £200
Users, Non-users and Potential Users Survey, Direct Mail Information
Service, £300
Business Direct Mail – Qualitative Research, Direct Mail Information Service,
£150
Business to Business Catalogues Research 1994, Direct Mail Information
Service, 1994, £150
Consumer Survey, Direct Mail Information Service, £250
Business to Business Direct Mail Trends, Direct Mail Information Service, £250

The Direct Mail Information Service also produces a number of extracts
from the above reports free of charge.

The Letterbox Factfile, Direct Mail Information Service, free
The Ready Reckoner (Dun Humby Associates), Institute of Direct Marketing,
1995, members £17.50, non-members £19.50
Building Brands Through Direct Marketing, 1995, Institute of Direct Marketing,
members £10.95, non-members £14.95
The Practitioner's Guide to Direct Marketing, Institute of Direct Marketing,
1992, members £75, non-members £95

Advertising

Quarterly Summary of Radio Listening, March–June 1997, RAJAR Ltd
Value For Money? The Chartered Insititute of Marketing, 1996
Manufacturing – The Marketing Solution, The Chartered Insititute of
Marketing,1995
Marketing – The Challenge of Change, The Chartered Insititute of Marketing,
1994
Advertising Means Business, The Advertising Association, 1997
The Radio Audience, Radio Joint Audience Research Limited (RAJAR), quar-
terly; annually: £650

Selling

1997 NatWest/BFA Franchise Survey, NatWest UK and the British Franchise
Association, 1997
The Two Partners of Franchising, by Peter Stern, Franchise World Directory, to
be published 1998
Behind the Veneer of Success: Propensities for UK Franchisor Failure, Small
Business Research Trust, 1997
Realising Your Export Potential, Barclays Bank plc Small Business
Services, 1996
Small Firms Survey – Exporting, British Chambers of Commerce, May 1997

The Facts - The UK Exhibition Industry, Volume 9, 1997, Exhibition Industry Federation, £85 inc. VAT

International Trade Manual, The British Chambers of Commerce, Sept. 1997, £35 inc. VAT

Quarterly Small Business Management Report, Vol. 3, No.4 – Pricing Policies, Lloyds Bank/Small Business Research Trust, November 1995.

Trade Fairs in Britain (calendar), Exhibition Industry Federation, annual: Oct., free

The NatWest/BFA Franchise Survey, NatWest, annual: Mar., £77.50

The NatWest/SBRT Survey of Exporters, Small Business Research Trust, tri-annual; annually: £40; each: £15;

Customer care

Consumer Creative Benchmarks. How Attititudes Towards Direct Mail Influence Response to Creative Work, Direct Mail Information Service, 1995

Improving Business Performance Through Service Excellence, MSB, 1997

MORI Research on Complaints Handling, carried out for the Citizen's Charter Unit, 1997

Raising the Standard, Institute of Management, Nov. 1994, £50

A 1995 Profile of Customer Survey Departments In The UK, TARP Europe Ltd, Dec. 1995, £50

Moving From Measuring To Managing Customer Satisfaction, TARP Europe Ltd, Jun. 1995, free

Project Insight – Results of an International Survey of Customer Satisfaction Programmes, 1993, £25, VA Research Ltd

Giving the right impression

Perfect Presentations, Khalid Aziz, The Aziz Coporation, 1997

The Effectiveness of PR in Local Newspapers, Welbeck Golin/Harris, £75

Issues and Crisis Management, Regester Larkin Ltd, 1996

A Survey of Developments in Issues Management, Regester Larkin Ltd, Nov. 1995, free

Employee Commitment and the Skills Revolution, Policy Studies Institute, June 1993, £9.95

Communicating or Just Making Pretty Shapes, Colin Wheildon, Newspaper Advertising Bureau of Australia, approx. £10

Type and Layout (an enlarged version of the above), Strathmoor Press, $24.95

General

Business Briefing, British Chambers of Commerce, weekly; annually: £94;

Small Firms Surveys: Innovation/R&D Environment Internationalisation

Competitiveness, Exporting, Training, British Chambers of Commerce, approx. every two months; each: £25

Meeting Business Needs in Britain, British Chambers of Commerce, July 1995, £25

Businesses Are Citizens of Europe, British Chambers of Commerce, July 1995, £10

State of the Market Report, Chartered Institute of Marketing, quarterly; annually: £12

Marketing Trends Survey, Chartered Institute of Marketing, quarterly; annually: £75

Metamorphosis in Marketing Report, Chartered Institute of Marketing, Spring 1993, £950

The Challenge of Change Report, Chartered Institute of Marketing, Spring 1994, £99

Journal of Marketing Management, The Dryden Press, 8 times per year, annually: £175

Advertising, Sponsorship and Promotions – Understanding and Measuring the Effectiveness of Commercial Sponsorship; Madrid, ESOMAR, Swiss Francs 110

Planning for Social Change 1996/97, The Henley Centre for Forecasting, July 1996, £9,500

Media Futures 1996/97, The Henley Centre for Forecasting, Oct. 1996, £11,000

Leisure Futures, The Henley Centre for Forecasting, quarterly £1,225

Planning Consumer Markets, The Henley Centre for Forecasting, Jan. 1996, £1,135

Consumer Markets 2000, The Henley Centre for Forecasting, Dec. 1995, £950.00

Teleculture 2000, The Henley Centre for Forecasting, Mar. 1994, £825

Lottery II, The Henley Centre for Forecasting, Nov. 1995, £550

Levers of Field Sales Productivity, Hewson Consulting Group Publications/ Mercatus, Mar. 1996, £225

Towards Excellence in Marketing Strategy – the Emerging Role of IT, Hewson Consulting Group Publications/Mercatus, Jan. 1996, £98

The Impact of Computerised Sales and Marketing Systems in the UK, Hewson Consulting Group Publications/Mercatus, Mar. 1994, £98

Emerging Information Technologies – A Marketing Opportunity (2nd edition), Hewson Consulting Group Publications/Mercatus, Aug. 1996, £98

The Media Guide, Institute of Direct Marketing, 1994, members: £75, non-members: £21.95

European Logistics Comparative Costs and Practice Survey, Institute of Logistics, 1997

Logisitics In Europe – The Vision and the Reality, Institute of Logistics, 1996

The Changing Role of Third Party Logistics – Can the Customer Ever Be Satisfied?, Institute of Logisitics, 1996

Quality and the Manager, Institute of Management, Dec. 1993, £30

Marketing, Institute of Management, May 1995, £15.99

Marketing for Non-marketing Managers, Institute of Management, May 1995, £15.99

The Single European Market – What's The Difference?, P-E International, Nov. 1995, £50

Supply Chain Partnerships – Who Wins?, P-E International, Nov. 1994, £40

Developing Supply Chain Relationships Throughout Europe, P-E International, Oct. 1995, £50

Contracting Out or Selling Out?, P-E International, Nov. 1993, £30

Going Green, P-E International, Jan. 1993, £30

Bolton Twenty Years On, Small Business Research Trust, 1991, £18.77

Lloyds Bank/SBRT, Quarterly Small Business Management Report, Small Business Research Trust, quarterly; annually: £55.00, each: £17.50

NatWest Review of Small Business Trends, Small Business Research Trust, bi-annual; annually: £55; each: £30

NatWest/SBRT Quarterly Survey of Small Business in Britain, Small Business Research Trust, quarterly; annually: £55, each: £17.50

ACKNOWLEDGEMENTS

We would like to thank the following people and organisations for their help and contributions in putting together this book.

ACAS
The Advertising Association
The Aziz Corporation
Barclays Bank plc Small Business Services
The Basic Skills Agency
Bemrose UK Ltd
The Drayton Bird Partnership
British Chambers of Commerce
British Franchise Association
British Telecom
Calcom Group Ltd
Chartered Institute of Marketing
Chartered Institute of Purchasing and Supply
Citizen's Charter Unit
The Direct Mail Information Service
The Direct Marketing Association
The Dryden Press
ESOMAR
European Journal of Marketing
Exhibition Industry Federation
John Fenton Training International plc
Hallmark Public Relations
Henley Centre for Forecasting
Hewson Consulting Group
The Institute of Direct Marketing
Institute of Logistics
Institute of Management Foundation

Journal of Marketing Management
The L & R Group
MCB University Press
McGraw-Hill Book Company Europe
Managing The Service Business (MSB)
National Consumer Council
National Dairy Council
NatWest UK
Newspaper Advertising Bureau of Australia
Office of Fair Trading
P-E International
Plain English Campaign
The Policy Studies Institute
Radio Advertising Bureau
RAJAR
Regester Larkin Ltd
The Research Business
Research Services Ltd
Richmond Events Ltd
Sales and Marketing Management
Small Business Research Trust
Strathmoor Press
The Survey Shop
TARP
VA Research
Welbeck Golin/Harris Communications Limited

ACKNOWLEDGEMENTS

Margaret Bennett,
  Bennett Unity
David Bernstein
Drayton Bird
Ken Burnett
Jacqui Canning
Marcus Child
Elaine Fenleigh
John Fenton
Ian Fletcher
John Goodwin

Gordon Greenley
Derek Holder
Louella Miles
Richard A Moore
Peter Mouncey
Philip Mounsey
Ken Peattie
Beverley Porter-Blake
Gordon A Presly
Arabella Price
Michael Regester

Bill Richards
Christine Rowat
Peter Scott-Smith
George Smith
Peter Stern
Merlin Stone
Judith Taylor
Nick Wells
Colin Wheildon
Brian Young

We would also like to thank Alison Alsbury for her work in preparing the second edition.

CONTENTS

direct mail? ▪ Is your mailshot going to irritate your prospects? ▪
What are the most common complaints about direct mail? ▪
Which types of direct mail generate the most complaints? ▪
How are your customers influenced by direct mail?

Are you honest? ▪ Does direct mail give a good impression of
your company? ▪ Does responding to direct mail affect your
customer's attitude to the company? ▪ Does getting direct mail
make your prospects more likely to buy from you? ▪ How important
to your company image do you think the practical factors are?
▪ How can you convince your prospects that you are a
reputable organisation?

First of all, who sends direct mail? ▪ What type of people get
the most direct mail? ▪ How many other pieces of direct mail are
you competing with? ▪ What sort of direct mail do consumers want?

How do consumers treat direct mail? ▪ What persuades people
to open the letters they receive from you? ▪ Are consumers more
likely to open the envelope if they know it's from you? ▪ Which
type of people are most likely to open and read your mailshot? ▪
How many people will keep your direct mail for future reference? ▪
Do people pass on direct mail?

What type of direct mail would influence you? ▪ How much
direct mail is wasted? ▪ Do people prefer to respond by phone
or by post? ▪ What reasons do people give for preferring to reply
by post? ▪ What are the most effective response options? ▪ How
about asking prospects to respond by fax? ▪ What does your
response method say about you?

What type of direct mail do consumers respond to? ▪ How often
do consumers respond to direct mail? ▪ How does the response
rate vary according to the type of response you want? ▪ Which
industries get the best response? ▪ Does the size of the mailing
affect the response rate? ▪ Will you get a better response if you
spend more? ▪ What type of responses do people make to direct
mail? ▪ How much can you influence the response rate by adapting
the mailshot?

ADVERTISING

customers ever say 'no' when they mean 'yes'? ■ How many times
do you have to be told 'no'? ■ What do buyers dislike most about
sales people?

EXPORTING 177

Who do you rely on for expertise in conducting your business abroad? ■ How much research is necessary? ■ What topics are usually researched? ■ Do you need specific training for exporting? ■ Is training really necessary? ■ What are the greatest barriers to overseas business? ■ How do you go about choosing an overseas agent or distributor?

Why export? 182

Why not? ■ Why are many businesses reluctant to export ■ What are the most common reasons for starting to export? ■ Is your business too small to export? ■ What makes small business exports fail? ■ Do you need to speak the language? ■ Which marketing activities promote exports? ■ How do you find out about overseas business opportunities? ■ Which regulatory factors influence your decision on which countries to do business with? ■ Which other factors influence your decision?

Credit control 189

How do you assess the creditworthiness of new overseas customers? ■ How do you ensure payments from your overseas buyers? ■ How serious is the problem of late payment by export customers?

EXHIBITING 191

Why should you exhibit? ■ Why do other companies exhibit ■ Are exhibitions an effective marketing medium? ■ How useful are exhibitions for launching new products? ■ For a successful exhibition, what are the most important things to plan? ■ How do you make a record of who visits the stand? ■ How long does it take to convert exhibition enquiries into sales?

Costs 196

What proportion of your marketing budget goes on exhibitions? ■ What is your annual exhibitions budget? ■ Where does the money go?

Exhibition visitors 198

Why do people visit exhibitions? ■ What action do people take as a result of visiting exhibitions?

you to answer the phone? ■ Who answers your careline number?
■ Do you ask callers for their name and address? ■ Are consumers
happy with the standard of carelines? ■ Do your competitors'
products carry a careline number?

Do you make specific commitments to your customers about
customer care standards? ■ What's wrong with service in shops? ■
How likely are customers to buy from you again after experiencing
a problem with your customer service? ■ Why do customers switch
their allegiance to one of your competitors?

Why do customers return goods to shops for an exchange or
refund? ■ How would customers prefer to approach you if they
have a complaint about a product bought from a shop? ■ How
many of your customers do not contact you when confronted with
a problem? ■ Do your customers keep their dissatisfaction to
themselves because they are nervous of complaining? ■ What
do people hope to gain by complaining? ■ What are consumers'
biggest serious complaints? ■ How many people will you
customers tell about their experience?

Does it matter how quickly you respond to the complaint? ■ Does
it make a difference how many times the customer has to contact
you to resolve the problem? ■ What do consumers think are the
most important factors in handling a complaint? ■ How much
does it cost your organisation to deal with complaints? ■ Who
deals with letters of complaint?

Does loyalty affect attitudes towards direct mail? ■ Does
personalising the message acknowledge the relationship?

Are your supply chain relationships crucial to customer care? ■
What do supply chain relationships require? ■ Who drives outbound
supply chains? ■ Who drives inbound supply chains? ■ How willing
are companies to discuss logistics costs openly with their partners? ■

What are the cost benefits of closer co-operation? ■ Why do companies outsource distribution? ■ What are the main problems about outsourcing? ■ What are the causes of these problems?

GIVING THE RIGHT IMPRESSION

How important is media image? ■ How important is it to get the creative right first time? ■ Will creative be affected by which sector you're in? ■ How will it affect your image if you write to your customers to keep them in touch with your organisation? ■ What effect are you having on business people if you send them inaccurate or duplicated mailshots?

How consistent are consumers in the types of products they buy? ■ Are people more likely to notice a new brand in some product areas than others? ■ How do consumers perceive own label products?

What does it cost to make sponsorship pay?

How much more likely to be seen and read is your editorial than your advertisements? ■ How can you make sure that your editorial hits the mark? ■ Which of the various types of editorial are most likely to be read? ■ Which types of editorial in local newspapers get most read? ■ How much does editorial reading in local papers vary by different subjects? ■ Does branded, PR-led editorial get less read than magazine originated editorial? ■ Does branded editorial in local papers get less read than all editorial? ■ Does a magazine add believability to branded editorial? And does it vary between magazines? ■ Does a newspaper add believability to branded editorial? Does it vary between papers?

How can you improve your handling of the media?

Crisis management

255

What are the most common mistakes in crisis planning? ■ What are the key steps for successful crisis planning? ■ What are the most common mistakes in crisis handling? ■ What are the key steps for successful crisis handling?

PUBLIC RELATIONS

257

Measuring the effectiveness of PR

257

How can you assess the value of your PR?

Using an agency

259

On what basis do you pay your PR agency? ■ How often should you review your relationship with your PR agency?

Internal PR

260

How are employees told about what goes on at their place of work, and are they able to give feedback? ■ Are employees satisfied with the level of communication they receive? ■ What forms of internal communication increase employee satisfaction with communication levels? ■ What is the most effective channel for communication? ■ How many companies have internal magazines or newsletters? ■ Are internal communications improving?

SALES PROMOTIONS

264

Christmas gifts

264

What sort of Christmas gifts should you give your customers? ■ How much do you spend on Christmas gifts?

Competitions

265

How much do you spend on prizes, and how many do you give? ■ How can you make sure your competition is a success?

Using an agency

267

On what basis do you pay your sales promotion agency? ■ How often should you review your relationship with your sales promotion agency?

DESIGN, PRINT AND THE WRITTEN WORD

268

Layout

268

How can you design the layout of a page to encourage people to read it? ■ How can you encourage people to read the text? ■ Which are best – photos or illustrations? ■ Should you justify text?

Readability

Do people find serif or sans serif type easier to read? ■ Do people find capitals or lower case letters more legible? ■ Is emboldened text easier or harder to read? ■ Are italics harder to read? ■ Which styles of headline type are easiest to read? ■ Which type sizes are easiest to read as continuous text? ■ Does kerning affect legibility (and what is it, anyway)? ■ How legible is 'reversed out' text? ■ How easy is it to read black text on a grey background? ■ Do people find it easier to read from matt or gloss paper?

Colour

Are your targets more likely to read and understand headlines in coloured type? ■ How easy is it to read text on a tinted background? ■ How will your readers respond to coloured text? ■ Is it worth paying for spot colour in an ad?

Language

How can you be sure that your writing style is clear?

INTRODUCTION

This is a business reference book with a difference. The information it contains is directly useful to you and your business. There's a lot of statistical material currently available, but it tends to be industry-specific or whole industry figures. It's not terribly helpful to know what's going on in the baked bean industry if you run a chain of travel agencies. And knowing what the total UK advertising spend is each year tells you precious little about your own advertising budget.

This book will give you generic – not industry-specific – business data, so it will apply to you whatever business you're in. It starts with the questions you might reasonably ask, and tries to answer them.

All the information in this book is relevant to the UK. Businesses overseas do some things very differently, and building their research information into the results would dilute the accuracy of the figures. The book gives you average data for the individual organisation, so you can see how it compares with yours.

You can use *The Essential Marketing Sourcebook* for four main purposes:

- **Benchmarking**: you'll find plenty of information about how other businesses conduct various marketing activities, and you can measure your own performance against the average.

- **Planning**: before you launch into a new initiative, you can look through the relevant section to see what the key factors are to consider. For example, if you're thinking of installing a computerised sales and marketing system, you'll find that the relevant section of this book will tell you what the most common pitfalls are, and what are the key ingredients for success.

> The book gives you average data for the individual organisation, so you can see how it compares with yours.

- **Decision making**: you'll find the answers to all sorts of questions here, to help you reach decisions. Suppose you want to advertise in the local paper, and you want to position the ad on the page that is most likely to be read. The relevant section of this book will tell you which page of the local paper is read by the most people.

- **Supporting proposals and presentations:** the information in this book comes from reliable and authoritative sources. Consequently you will find it invaluable for adding weight to your own arguments. Suppose you want to persuade the board of directors that they should invest

> You'll find the answers to all sorts of questions here, to help you reach decisions.

more in customer retention, rather than focusing on winning new customers. After referring to this book, you will be able to inform them that recruiting new customers costs between three and seven times more than hanging on to the ones you've already got.

The Essential Marketing Sourcebook pulls together information on marketing topics from planning and strategy through to leaflet design, calling in on research, direct marketing, advertising, selling, customer care, PR, sales promotion and others along the way. It should quickly become one of the most well-thumbed books on your shelf.

The series

This book is one of *The Essential Business Sourcebooks*. The other book in the series is *The Essential Personnel Sourcebook*. They cover two vital aspects of business, and have proved immensely popular. The second editions carry updated material where relevant, and extend their coverage to reflect new developments in the last few years. Gurus – leading industry specialists – have also kindly contributed to the second editions, so they include a wealth of practical advice from people in the know.

You may find that certain topics you are interested in are included in the other book. For example negotiation, which you might reasonably consider to be an aspect of marketing, has been included in *The Essential Personnel Sourcebook* since most of the information available on the subject relates to personnel issues.

However, where only one or two pieces of data overlap between the books, we have included them in both books to make it easier for you to find them. For instance, you will find that the section of this book on internal PR also appears in *The Essential Personnel Sourcebook*.

The data

We have used only the most reliable data we could find in this series of books. Clearly the methodology varies widely between studies, but if we included the full details of it each time, there would be no room to include the findings. Each piece of data is clearly sourced where it appears in the text, and you will find a complete list of contact details at the back of the book (Appendix II) should you wish to find out more.

We have studied the data ourselves, of course, and we have not included any material that we consider to be unreliable. In a few cases, we felt that the information available needed to be treated with a measure of caution. In these instances, we have made this view clear in the surrounding text. We took the view, however, that any information is more useful than no information, as long as you are aware of the possible risks in treating it as gospel. Where we felt that data were seriously flawed or biased, we excluded them.

The research findings included in the series are the most up-to-date we could find. In the vast majority of cases the research was published within the last three or four years. In a few cases the research is older than this, but often the reason no one has updated it is precisely because they do not expect it to have changed. We have not included any information that we considered to be unreliable because of its age.

The Essential Business Sourcebooks are a comprehensive guide to useful UK business data. But since the series is based on research data, we are obviously limited by the research that is available. We have found useful material on all the major areas of business, but it is possible that you may be interested in a particular aspect of one of these areas that you cannot find listed in the contents. If this happens, it will be because (after months of research, and contacts with hundreds of organisations) we have failed to track down any reliable data on the subject. If you know of any survey or other research data that is relevant to this series but which we have not included, we would be very pleased to hear from you so that we can include it in the next edition.

The contributors

The data in these books have been contributed by many of the most highly respected institutes and research organisations, by government departments, and by some of the top experts in various fields. We are very grateful to them for their co-operation.

Some of the reports that we have taken extracts from are publicly available from these organisations. In most cases, we have reproduced only a small part of the full research findings – the information we think will be of the widest interest. But if you have a special interest in any subject, you may well want to see the full report. A listing of surveys and reports that are published

> **The data have been contributed by many of the most highly respected institutes and research organisations.**

by our contributing organisations appears at the front of this book. This listing not only includes the reports from which we have taken extracts, but also gives details of any other reports and surveys that you might find interesting.

How to use the book

The book is divided into broad marketing categories (for example 'direct marketing'), which are subdivided into more specific categories (such as 'telemarketing'). These are then divided further into areas within this (for example 'costs'). Finally, the data in these sections have been split into individual subject areas, each headed with a question (e.g. How much does telemarketing cost per call?). You will find a very comprehensive contents list at the front of the book, to help you find your way around this system.

We have presented each piece of data in the form which illustrates it most clearly. In many cases, this involves using charts, graphs, matrices and other things that make some people feel slightly unnerved and confused. If you're one of these people, you may find Appendix I helpful. It is a user-friendly guide to reading statistics which briefly explains each type of graph, chart and figure that you may come across while using the book. Let me reassure you, however, that we have not tried to be clever, but have used only those graphics which are in relatively common use.

Although we have designed the books to be functional, we were surprised when we put them together to find just how fascinating much of the research material is, even when the subject matter is not immediately relevant to you. You should find it easy to track down the information you want; we hope however that you will find the book sufficiently interesting that you will not only use it for its primary purpose – as a reference book – but will also find it entertaining to browse through for general interest.

> **We were surprised to find just how fascinating much of the research material is.**

PLANNING AND PREPARATION

PLANNING

Marketing processes

■ *What aspects of marketing should you plan?*

This is the first question to ask when you start to look at any marketing operation. But how do you go about answering it? One good way to start is by looking at what other businesses do. The Chartered Institute of Marketing's survey *Manufacturing – The Marketing Solution* surveyed 44 manufacturing companies across the UK. One of its aims was to develop a valid framework that UK manufacturing companies can use to benchmark their performance through marketing. The survey identified seven separate marketing processes:

The 7 separate marketing processes
1 Marketing strategy
2 Quality strategy
3 Innovation
4 Customer development
5 Branding
6 Supply chain management
7 Manufacturing strategy

The survey then developed a series of objective yes/no questions for each process which could be used to give each company an objective score of its performance.

■ *How well does your company perform in each part of the marketing process?*

Having divided marketing into these seven processes, how much does performance vary between each? You could be really hot on manufacturing strategy but hopeless when it comes to branding. (If this is the case, you're not alone.) The surveyed companies performed far better in some areas than others. On average, the companies were best at manufacturing strategy, and noticeably poorest at branding. Each company was marked on a scale of 1 (poor) to 5 (excellent) for each of the seven processes.

Business process	1	2	3	4	5	Average score
Marketing strategy	9%	30%	32%	23%	7%	2.9
Quality strategy	18%	16%	20%	23%	23%	3.1
Branding	66%	16%	14%	4%	_	1.5
Innovation	14%	20%	29%	20%	16%	3.0
Customer development	9%	25%	23%	32%	11%	3.1
Supply chain management	14%	20%	29%	18%	18%	3.0
Manufacturing strategy	9%	20%	25%	23%	23%	3.3

Source: Manufacturing – The Marketing Solution, Chartered Institute of Marketing survey, 1995

■ How much effect does each marketing process have on business success?

Does it really make much difference to the bottom line how well you do in all these areas? The survey measured which of the seven manufacturing processes were related to business success, which they measured in terms of return on sales. They found that performance in five of these areas correlated significantly with business success:

1 Marketing strategy

2 Innovation

3 Customer development

4 Branding

5 Supply chain management

Source: Manufacturing – The Marketing Solution, Chartered Institute of Marketing survey, 1995

3

■ Can marketing processes be used to evaluate marketing performance?

Knowing which processes affect marketing success is one thing. Measuring marketing performance is another. Is it possible to find a way to measure marketing success? The Chartered Institute of Marketing has developed a framework for doing just this in the retail sector. Marketing strategy should be integrative, providing a direction and a focus for the business. Supply chain management and the management of operations are also relevant to performance, so they have been included in the framework.

Marketing excellence framework

Marketing Strategy

Supply Chain Management

Branding

New Product Development

Customer Development

Operations

Business Performance

Quality Strategy

Source: Are We Being Served? Chartered Institute of Marketing, 1997

■ How can you score your marketing performance?

The Chartered Institute of Marketing takes the seven processes mentioned above, and splits them into their component parts. Your company can then score itself on the basis of each component in terms of competitive marketing performance. The main components of each process are:

Marketing strategy

- Review of company's competitive position
- Systematic process for the collection and use of market information
- Involvement of all levels of staff in collecting market information
- Explicit strategies for development and management of strategic alliances
- Development of resources explicitly linked to market information
- Organisational structures reflecting the marketing strategy

Quality strategy

- Commitment of top management to quality
- Long-term commitment of company to quality
- Culture which underpins quality
- Personnel issues seen as critical to implementation of quality strategies

Branding

- Clear understanding of role of brands throughout business
- Branding seen as source of competitive advantage
- Brand management structures reinforce marketing performance

New product development

- New product development seen as critical to business success
- Systematic approaches to new product development
- External stakeholders deliberately involved in new product development
- Product and process development are simultaneous considerations
- Cross-functional teams deliberately involved in new product development
- New product development is time driven
- Quantified goals are established to manage and control new product development performance

Customer development

- Conscious explicit approach to segmentation, targeting and positioning
- Company explicitly manages through relationship marketing
- Explicit distribution strategies
- Strategic approach to customer service staff management
- Effective management of pricing decisions
- Communications mix effectively managed

Supply chain management

- Supply chain management has a strategic role
- Explicit systems for managing suppliers
- Appropriate organisational structure for effective purchasing
- Supply chain management is customer-focused
- Company and suppliers share same strategic vision

Operations

- Operations strategic role is recognised
- Operations strategy is determined by explicit reference to market needs and competitive activity
- Operations strategy is determined with reference to location and physical environment.

Source: Are We Being Served? Chartered Institute of Marketing, 1997

■ *How can you expect the rate of technical change in the industry to affect performance?*

You would expect that having to accommodate fast-changing technology would have an impact on performance. But would you expect it to be a positive or a negative impact? Interestingly, it seems to depend on where the changes are happening – in the supply market, in the products, or in the manufacturing technology.

With seven processes and a maximum score of five in each, the highest overall score possible for each company in the survey was 35.

The total scores were plotted against competitive performance (measured as a ratio of profit before interest and tax on turnover (PBIT) to sales turnover) with the following results:

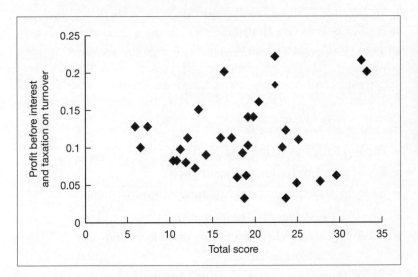

There are a couple of points worth noting here:

1 Large companies were significantly more likely to appear in the low performing–high scoring position.

2 High performers/high scorers were significantly more likely to operate in markets where there is a high rate of technical change:

- 36% of high performers faced high rates of technical change in their supply markets. None of the low performers' supply markets was changing rapidly.

- 50% of high performers operated in markets with high rates of product change (compared with only 12% of low performers).

- By contrast, a high rate of change in manufacturing technologies was linked to low performance: 81% of companies with slow rates of change in manufacturing technology were high performers, compared with 55% of companies with rapid change in manufacturing technologies.

Source: Manufacturing – The Marketing Solution, Chartered Institute of Marketing survey, 1995.

IT in marketing planning

■ *What is a marketing planning system?*

If your planning hasn't moved into the 21st century yet, you may well be unsure about exactly how you can use a computerised system to help you. In fact, some systems feed into the planning process, while others actually carry out specific planning tasks. Broadly, there are five different functions that a marketing system can perform, all of which can contribute to, or help with, the job of planning. The five roles of IT in marketing are:

1 To store, retrieve, analyse and present data on customers, products, markets, channels and the competition.

2 To provide immediate access to information at the customer interface or internally.

3 To reduce the paperwork involved in passing data through the supply chain.

4 To perform tasks such as building product quotations, planning and scheduling sales calls, keeping diaries, reporting on the progress of marketing campaigns, compiling mailshots and routeing telephone calls.

5 To provide and reinforce controls, procedures and best practice, for example by checking that certain stages of a process have been carried out.

Source: Hewson Consulting Group

■ *How can you make sure that you get the best from your system?*

Of course, just because you have a system in place, doesn't necessarily mean that it will be a resounding success. You need to select and use the system in the optimum way in order to get the best results from it. But how do you do this? Hewson Consulting researched the answers to this question by reviewing published literature and interviewing 60 managers from 30 organisations. They found that there were thirteen critical success factors in choosing and using a marketing planning system.

13 critical success factors

1 **Market orientation:** unless your organisation sees a need to increase market orientation, marketing planning is unlikely to be accepted.

2 **Absence of excessive short-term pressures:** if there are so many of these pressures that managers haven't the time or motivation for strategic planning, you won't get the best from your system.

3 **Presence of a system champion and sponsor:** you need people to fill these two roles – a champion to drive the process of introducing the system, and a senior-level sponsor to provide a supportive environment.

4 **System perceived as empowering, not controlling.**

5 **Sufficiently wide team definition:** the planning team needs to be sufficiently wide to embrace the relevant functions, and sufficiently senior to act on the insights reached. Obtaining these people's input on paper is less successful than obtaining their active involvement.

6 **Adequate training.**

7 **A good facilitator:** these people help to manage time and organise training. They should be knowledgeable about marketing theory, cautious with advice and open with knowledge.

8 **Co-ordinating use of the system with the planning cycle.**

9 **Appropriate planning units:** the definition of the business unit and its component products and markets are crucial. It is important not to follow an inappropriate organisational plan, such as a product-based one.

10 **Flexibility in planning processes.**

11 **Garbage in, garbage out:** the system's outputs are determined by the user's inputs. Until this is recognised, users may doubt the value of the system.

12 **Development should be expert-driven as well as user-driven:** developers and future users may not be well versed in relevant marketing theory, so involving experts in developing the system ensures that it embodies 'best practice'.

13 **Use prototyping:** this area of software development is still fairly new, and it tends to take more than one attempt to customise the system to fit the individual organisation – so be prepared for this.

Source: Hewson Consulting Group

Marketing strategy

■ *What help can you get in putting together your marketing strategy?*

There are various decision making methods you can use to help you draw up a strategic marketing plan. But do other companies really use these techniques? In their study *Marketing Planning Decision Making in UK and US Companies*, Gordon E Greenley and Barry L Bayus investigated which of these methods are being used. They also found out how many of the respondents regularly use each technique, and how many have tried but abandoned each one. The UK findings only are reproduced here.

Decision making method	Regularly use	Tried, no longer use	Heard of, never used	Heard of, appropriate	Never heard of
SWOT analysis	54%	7%	14%	8%	12%
Portfolio analysis	42%	8%	21%	12%	11%
PLC analysis	51%	11%	20%	9%	5%
PIMS	5%	5%	30%	14%	42%
Perceptual mapping	12%	8%	25%	15%	36%
Conjoint analysis	5%	5%	20%	13%	53%
Qualitative judgement	55%	9%	13%	9%	9%

Source: Journal of Marketing Management

■ *What sort of information do you need for effective strategic planning?*

It depends on what exactly you're planning, of course. But are you feeding in all the information you could possibly need? Are you utilising as wide a range of data as, say, your competitors are using in their planning process? Greenley and Bayus asked their respondents what information they were inputting to four different aspects of marketing planning.

Information input	Pricing products	Advertising budgets	Launching new products	Eliminating products
Focus groups	41%	35%	58%	48%
Internal data	90%	77%	76%	78%
Observation	70%	54%	73%	70%
Personal judgement	88%	87%	80%	75%
Surveys	33%	21%	59%	51%
Test marketing	29%	18%	68%	37%
Laboratory experiments	2%	2%	14%	7%
Panel data	17%	9%	18%	7%
Other syndicate data	20%	13%	23%	16%
Competitive data	88%	52%	86%	74%
Industry association data	48%	35%	50%	41%
Government data	31%	14%	44%	32%

Source: *Journal of Marketing Management*

■ *Is your strategic planning effective enough? And if not, what can you do about it?*

You may not feel that your strategic planning process needs any improvement (although you'd be in the minority if you did). But if it does, do you need different information or do you simply need better analysis of the data you already have? Greenley and Bayus asked this question in order to focus on the best way of improving the effectiveness of decision making in marketing planning.

Decision	Improved analysis	Alternative data	No improvement needed
Pricing products	59%	43%	20%
Setting advertising budgets	65%	31%	21%
Launching new products	66%	45%	16%
Eliminating products	61%	35%	19%

Source: *Journal of Marketing Management*

■ *What makes a good strategic plan?*

Once you have gathered all your information, and you're ready to put together your strategic plan, how can you be sure of making it as effective as possible? These are the criteria for a good strategic plan; the list was put together with reference to direct marketing, but it applies to any strategic marketing plan.

The 6 qualities of a good strategic plan
1 Easy to understand
2 Precise but detailed, to avoid confusion
3 Adaptable to change
4 Realistic in application
5 Covers all significant market factors
6 Clearly identifies responsibilities

Source: The Practitioner's Guide to Direct Marketing, The Institute of Direct Marketing, 1992

■ *How long does it take to plan and execute a campaign effectively?*

Are you one of those people who always finds themselves wishing that they'd got started on each project earlier? If so, join the club. But why are most of us inclined to rush campaigns, at least to some extent? Often it's really not our fault. It's because we haven't a clue how long each stage should take and how early we *should* have started planning. So here is a general guide to timescale for some of the more frequent marketing campaigns.

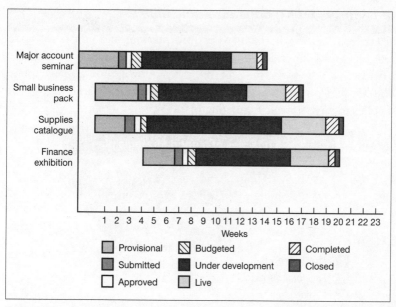

Source: *The Practitioner's Guide to Direct Marketing*, The Institute of Direct Marketing, 1992

SMALL FIRMS

■ *Does your small firm plan its marketing strategy?*

If it does, the outlook is positive. Barclays researched 400 small businesses, looking at the issue of business planning. The research showed that businesses which plan are more optimistic about the future and more ambitious than those that don't. They are also more likely to take advice, more likely to undertake training, and, as a result, more likely to achieve profitable growth.

Source: *Planning To Keep One Step Ahead*, Barclays Bank plc Small Business Services, September 1996

■ *How many small businesses plan?*

Having committed time, energy and resources to setting up a business, many businesses are failing to plan adequately. Only three in ten small businesses have a formal business plan – well over one third have no plan at all!

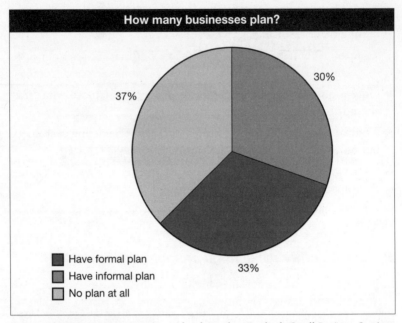

How many businesses plan?

30%

37%

33%

- Have formal plan
- Have informal plan
- No plan at all

Source: Planning To Keep One Step Ahead, Barclays Bank plc Small Business Services, September 1996

■ *Do other small firms get their marketing strategy right?*

If you are experiencing problems with your marketing strategy, are you alone? Not according to Mike Davis of Barclays Bank:

> *Research among small business shows that loss of market and lack of sales are two of the main problems they face. Many of the half a million small businesses which close every year may do so because entrepreneurs have neither identified their markets properly, nor researched the competition, especially at the crucial early stage prior to starting up.*

Source: Mike Davis, Small Business Services Director, Barclays Bank plc

■ *Are other small firms good at marketing?*

So how are your competitors faring? Do other small firms have a good track record in marketing? It would appear that the answer is no.

- Small businesses spend on average £1,500 a year on marketing, yet fewer than 4 in 10 measure the effectiveness of the activities undertaken.

- 8 out of 10 small businesses spend less than 5 hours a week promoting their business.

- 7 out of 10 entrepreneurs do not carry out market research prior to starting up, and, over time, even less planning activity is done.

- Only a quarter of small businesses properly calculate what they should charge to cover their costs.

- 7 out of 10 small businesses keep a database of existing customers, but only 1 in 10 use it to secure future business.

- Over two-thirds of small businesses do not see the need to change their approach to marketing in the future.

Source: Marketing and The Small Firm, Barclays Bank plc Small Business Services, May 1997

■ *How do other small firms promote their products?*

Promotion plays an important part in shaping a business's image. It need not be expensive – good public relations can be undertaken in-house, and rely on an investment of time rather than money. However, nearly two-thirds of businesses still rely on word of mouth or reputation, rather than considering the wider range of promotional tactics available.

Types of promotional activity undertaken	
Word of mouth/reputation	60%
Advertising in business directories	30%
Advertising in local press	30%
Advertising in trade/business press	12%
Direct mail	11%
Brochures/leaflets/point of sale material	5%
Local radio advertising	4%
Posters/vehicle sides/branding	4%
National press/TV advertising	3%
Telephone contact/personal visits	5%
Sponsorship	2%
Seminars/conferences/exhibitions	4%
PR	1%

Source: Marketing and The Small Firm, Barclays Bank plc Small Business Services, May 1997

■ *How do other businesses target existing customers?*

Increasing sales from existing customers is often a better use of resources than targeting new ones. Nine out of 10 entrepreneurs believe that the most appropriate way to target existing customers is to give the best possible service. But there are other low cost ways to strengthen relationships.

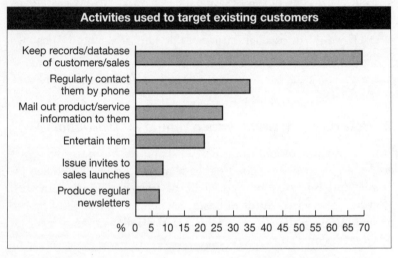

Source: Marketing and The Small Firm, Barclays Bank plc Small Business Services, May 1997

■ *What skills do you need to be good at marketing?*

Small firms were asked which skills they considered most vital for effective marketing. Knowledge of the product and the market topped the bill.

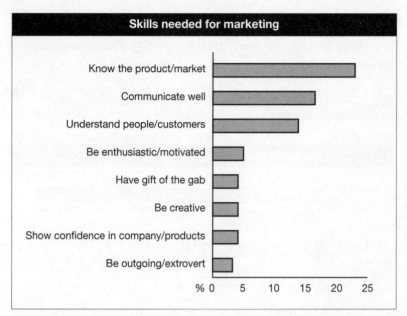

Skills needed for marketing

Know the product/market
Communicate well
Understand people/customers
Be enthusiastic/motivated
Have gift of the gab
Be creative
Show confidence in company/products
Be outgoing/extrovert

% 0   5   10   15   20   25

Source: Marketing and The Small Firm, Barclays Bank plc Small Business Services, May 1997

ADVICE

■ *Where do you go for advice?*

The traditional sources of business planning advice are accountants and banks. In addition to their expert financial advice, banks now provide market surveys and marketing advice. Chambers of Commerce provide vital local information. There is also a variety of business support organisations – Business Links, Training and Enterprise Councils, Enterprise Agencies. Much of the information provided by all these bodies is free.

Source: Planning To Keep One Step Ahead, Barclays Bank plc Small Business Services, September 1996

PLANNING AND PREPARATION

■ *Who provides which kind of advice?*

If you want a particular kind of advice, it will help to know who to approach for what:

Source	Range of advice available
Accountants	Professional advice on financial control and business planning
Banks	Assistance on practical and formal steps of developing a business plan
Business Links	Teams of Personal Business Advisers (PBAs) offer a wide range of business planning support services
Chambers of Commerce	A range of information services, seminars, training and education
Enterprise Agencies	Advice for start-up businesses on training and business planning
Training and Enterprise Councils (TECs)	Government agencies offering free or subsidised advice and training on business planning to small and medium-sized enterprises

Source: *Planning to Keep One Step Ahead*, Barclays Bank plc Small Business Services, September 1996

■ *Which sources of advice are most often used?*

Larger businesses either have a wealth of in-house expertise, or employ consultants. The majority of small businesses appear to be missing out on the wealth of practical information available. Barclays Bank's Small Business Services found many small businesses took advice only on financial matters:

Advice on business planning				
	Marketing/ advertising	Business planning	Cash flow/ financial control	Obtaining finance
No one	73%	57%	22%	32%
Banks	1%	12%	6%	56%
Accountants	3%	15%	58%	13%
Relatives/ colleagues	7%	4%	6%	4%
Consultants	2%	1%	1%	4%
TECs/Business Links	2%	7%	1%	2%

Source: *Planning to Keep One Step Ahead*, Barclays Bank plc Small Business Services, September 1996

■ Are there pitfalls which you can avoid by planning?

Drayton Bird, who founded the Drayton Bird Partnership, has the following six hints for those planning a new marketing drive, or launching into marketing for the first time.

1 **Never spend money without testing first**
   Most people think in terms of comparative testing. The most important – and easiest – test is often ignored: try out a message on small numbers before you spend all your money.

2 **Be careful when reading research**
   People can tell you: what they know; what they think; what they understand; what they don't know; what they think you want to hear. They cannot tell you what they will do.

3 **Beware focus group results**
   Small numbers mean samples cannot be statistically significant; strong individuals within them sway opinions; researchers can put a spin on results. Above all, what people say and what they do are very different. This is particularly true of long copy (they say they don't read it); free offers (they claim they're not influenced) and direct mail (they say they never open it).

19

4 Get your priorities right

A poor message sent to the right prospect is better than the other way round. No product, however brilliant, will sell to the wrong people. No creative treatment, however stunning, will succeed if it is not seen by the right ones.

5 Never forget the two questions that your prospect has in mind

- What will it do for me that nothing else can?
- Can it do something better than anything else?

6 The customer you want is like the customer you've got

This maxim should always guide your planning – unless, of course, you're a new firm.

Source: Drayton Bird, The Drayton Bird Partnership

MARKET RESEARCH

The cost of market research

■ *What does it cost to commission market research?*

If you need some market research into an area of your business, can you afford to commission it? Or can you afford to do it yourself cost effectively? Clearly it depends on the nature of the research. But the first thing you'll need to have is some idea of the cost of different types of market research commissions.

A 1994 study asked research institutes to give quotations for six research projects, and then calculated the average cost of each project. This gives a useful guideline as to the kind of ball park figure you'd be looking at for each type of commissioned research. The six projects included:

- Three consumer research projects (two based on face-to-face and one on telephone interviewing).

- Two consumer qualitative research projects (one based on group discussions and one on depth interviews).

- One business-to-business research project (telephone interviewing).

Here is an outline of each project and the average cost of commissioning each one.

Project 1	A national usage and attitude study on a chocolate confectionery product conducted via face-to-face interviewing among a quota sample of 750 adults (including 6 copies of a 45-page report).	£21,164
Project 2	A national telephone tracking study on washing powders among a quota sample of 500 housewives.	£10,307
Project 3	An in-home product usage test among an initial sample of 200 adult regular users of a dairy food product.	£9,981
Project 4	Four group discussions among consumers who are regular users of certain banking services.	£8,572
Project 5	Twenty depth interviews with consumers who are regular users of certain banking services.	£7,552
Project 6	A business-to-business telephone survey comprising 200 interviews with executives responsible for authorising the purchase/acquisition of office photocopiers.	£11,280

Source: *International Prices Study*, European Society for Opinion and Marketing Research (ESOMAR) 1994

Incidentally, ESOMAR repeated this price study across about 60 countries, and compared the results. The UK market research industry's prices turned out to be almost exactly average, and the 7th most expensive out of 15 Western European countries.

PLANNING AND PREPARATION

■ *What are the relative costs of different survey methods?*

Today's computers are so powerful that the time it takes to zap through a few thousand responses may be only a little longer than the time it takes to process a few hundred. This means that the fixed costs of designing and testing the questionnaire, setting up the analysis, and presenting the results, can have more of an impact on your final bill than the cost of the data analysis itself, even with a large survey. You can see the effect of this in the following table, which shows the approximate relative costs from initial planning to presentation of results:

Relative costs of survey methods					
Questionnaires completed	Survey data analysis	Telephone survey	Voluntary mailed response*	Face-to-face survey	Domestic survey
100	1.0	3.4	5 to 15+	3.2	8.6
500	1.7	11.6		10.1	37.0
1000	2.6	18.6		15.4	69.3
5000	9.6	92.3		71.1	34.0

*Considerable variation can be expected
Source: The Survey Shop

Questionnaires

■ *How long does it take to conduct a telephone survey?*

Conducting your own market research is perfectly possible, at least for the less specialist approaches, and can be very cost effective. However, you will need to cost it first, to make sure that you couldn't commission the research more cheaply. And one of the biggest costs you'll have to consider is staff time. Conducting your own in-house telephone surveys is perfectly feasible and can be very useful, even with quite a small survey base. But how much time should you expect it to take up?

● To achieve a specific number of respondents in telephone surveys, you will need to start with a list of at least twice that number.

- Telephone surveys vary in terms of the time they take. Just getting hold of the right person on the phone can take ages, before you even start to interview them. The range is from less than one successful interview per hour (for surveys of professionals and senior managers) to more than 12 per hour (for domestic customers).

- Estimate the time each interview should last by testing the questions on colleagues or other guinea pigs, and then doubling the time it takes. (This is because respondents in the survey will answer at greater length – even to yes and no questions – in order to explain why they make particular choices.)

Source: The Survey Shop

■ How can you minimise the cost of analysing questionnaire responses?

As we've seen, the cost of analysis may not vary much between small and large surveys. But it is still a significant factor in the overall cost, so it's worth bearing in mind the cost implications at the design stage.

- Tick-box responses are far cheaper and easier to analyse than open questions. However, they are less effective for eliciting new information and gauging the strength of opinions and feelings. If you need to use open questions, you may still be able to keep the cost down if you can use some tick-box responses.

- Use as few sides of paper as possible, to cut the time it takes to process the data. Turning pages can take almost as long as entering data. Single or double-sided sheets are far easier to handle (and therefore far cheaper to process) than folded or stapled sheets.

Source: The Survey Shop

■ What response should you expect to a business-to-business survey?

If you know how many replies you want, you need to know the response rate in order to calculate how many questionnaires to mail out in the first place.

- Survey response rates differ hugely, but in the business-to-business sector you can regard a response of between 5% and 15% as a success.

Source: The Survey Shop

■ *What sort of response can you expect to a consumer survey?*

This will, of course, vary widely. You will get a better response from your own customer list than from a cold mailing, for example.

● Depending on these factors, the normal range is between 12 and 70%.

Source: The Drayton Bird Partnership

■ *What techniques can you use to maximise the response to a postal survey?*

There's plenty you can do to boost your response rate, and in many cases research has established the likely percentage by which your response will increase as a result.

Technique to increase response rate	Percentage response increase
A clean customer file for sample selection	+ 150
First reminder (letter)	+ 26
Second reminder (phone)	+ 25
Introductory questions of high interest to respondents	+ 19
Relevant incentive	+ 18
Second reminder (letter + questionnaire + reply envelope)	+ 12
Second class post	+ 8
First class post	+ 5
Questionnaire on yellow paper	+ 4

Source: The Practitioner's Guide to Direct Marketing, The Institute of Direct Marketing, 1992

■ *What are the main dos and don'ts for planning and designing surveys?*

There is a wealth of received wisdom on the subject of survey design, and it can make a substantial difference to the number of replies you receive, and their quality and usefulness.

DOs

1 **Match questions to the original objectives.** Surveys can grow and grow if they are designed by committee, but overlong surveys are unpopular, and may be answered with less diligence (if at all).

2 **Consider the alternatives.** There are usually different ways to gather the same information. The telephone, fax, e-mail, postal service and face-to-face interview should all be on your list when you start to plan a survey.

3 **Make the most of opportunities to do a survey.** Trade events, group presentations, and normal customer contact all offer ways and means of cutting the cost of gathering data.

4 **Be aware of the pitfalls in using voluntary response postal surveys** – the respondents can be self-selecting. A national organisation recently achieved a creditable 23% response rate when they mailed out a detailed quality assurance questionnaire. However there is no way of knowing whether this 23% responded because they were more – or less – satisfied than the 77% who did not respond.

5 **Use surveys to build mailing lists.** In a showroom survey of 1,000 women, offered the opportunity to indicate that they did not want further information, only 36% took this option – creating a mailing list of 640 interested people.

6 **Effective postal surveys in the business-to-business sector depend on offering a worthwhile incentive and then making it as easy as possible to reply** (for example, pre-printed freepost envelopes). Successful incentives include entry into a draw for a luxury hamper, a donation to charity for each reply, a free gift, or a copy of the survey results.

PLANNING AND PREPARATION

DON'Ts

1 **Don't assume that you need thousands of respondents to get a useful result.** Put your efforts into gathering your data from a truly representative sample.

2 **Don't ask long or complicated questions.** Break everything down into the simplest possible set of components and test carefully before you begin. The worst source of confusion is usually branching questions (such as, if you have not bought a cheeseburger go to Q17b, otherwise go to Q15a).

3 **Don't assume that you have got all the right questions.** Use the occasional open question to discover the things that people might be bursting to tell you about the way they see it.

Source: The Survey Shop

BUDGETING

■ *How do you determine your marketing budget?*

Every year, you know you want to set aside a certain amount of money for marketing – that's what budgeting is all about, after all. But how on earth are you supposed to decide how much to earmark? The following survey focused on retailers, and started by examining how they set their marketing budget. As you can see, the majority used fairly unsophisticated methods, and almost a quarter said their method was arbitrary.

Method	Percentage of retailers using the method			
	Consumer nondurable	Consumer durable	Services	All
Percentage of anticipated sales	5	30	34.1	27
Availability of funds (affordable)	35	2	24.4	16.2
Objective/task	5	42	4.9	21.6
Arbitrary	25	20	29.3	24.3
Percentage of past years' sales	30	6	7.3	10.8

Source: European Journal of Marketing, 1990

■ *How long do you spend planning your marketing budget?*

The retailers surveyed above were also asked when they started planning their budget. As you can see, the good news is that, if you start budgeting just a few months ahead, you're already several steps ahead of most of the competition, at least if you work in the retailing industry.

Duration before start of financial year	Percentage of retailers using the method			
	Consumer nondurable	Consumer durable	Services	All
Over 6 months		6	14	7
4 to 6 months		7	2	
1 to 3 months		14	21	13
Less than 1 month	55	48	29	43
Not before start of financial year	45	32	29	28

Source: European Journal of Marketing, 1990

■ How do you decide what to spend your marketing budget on?

The sample retailers were asked which factors influenced their decisions on how to spend the budget. Several of the most important factors seem to be rather ad hoc, to say the least. Presumably this helps to explain why over a quarter of retailers in the survey still hadn't set their budgets at the start of their financial year, as we saw in the previous table.

Factor	Percentage*of retailers influenced			
	Consumer nondurable	Consumer durable	Services	All
Market conditions (sluggish/buoyant)	5	9	28	15
Effectiveness of source of expenditure based on experience	19	43	41	37
Competitors' actions	22	64	28	41
Availability of stock	38	22	10	21
Seasonal opportunity	24	36	31	32
Support from supplier/ manufacturer	5	6		4
Type of customer service need to be offered	16	4	17	12
Expected margin from the product/service		35		15
New product/ model/range		16	7	9
Size of market to be canvassed/covered		10	12	9

*Figures exceed 100% due to multiple responses

Source: European Journal of Marketing, 1990

DIRECT MARKETING

INTRODUCTION

■ What is direct marketing?

Direct marketing is a modern term for an age-old practice. Essentially, it is the process of recruiting and retaining customers by direct, two-way communication. You don't use an intermediary (such as a wholesaler or retailer) and you invite the prospect or customer to respond directly to you.

So direct marketing includes direct mail, telemarketing, mail order and direct advertising (any form of advertising that asks for a direct response). This chapter deals with all of these except for direct advertising, which is covered in the next chapter.

Any effective direct marketing operation relies heavily on building up an individual relationship with each customer. This means collecting and storing all the relevant information you can about each prospect and customer, and constantly updating it. For all but the most basic operations, this calls for a computerised system – a database of all your prospects and customers – which contains as many relevant details as possible about each one. Any form of marketing that takes its leads from such a system (both literally and metaphorically) is known as database marketing.

■ What do consumers think of direct marketing?

Attitudes vary widely to different forms of direct marketing. Consumers can be very positive about some aspects of it, and very negative about others. It is also wise to bear in mind that although the responses people give are probably a fairly accurate view of how they feel, their actions do not necessarily bear this out. For example, many people say that they hate to receive unsolicited mail, yet only a small fraction of them would bother to have themselves removed from a mailing list.

Response	Percentage agree	Percentage disagree
Strongly object to being rung up	90	6
Strongly object to being written to	68	20
Rarely read loose ads	64	28
Enjoy reading catalogues	52	37
Some advertising mail is useful and informative	48	42
Sometimes reply to competitions	39	56
Like companies writing to me about things which might interest me	37	49
Often cut out/send coupons	22	72

Source: Direct Mail Information Service, 1993

DIRECT MAIL

Techniques and targeting

■ *Are there any techniques which work particularly well?*

For each mailer, each campaign is unique. For the recipients each mailing is just one of many. Does the volume of the communication matter? Volume of content may have the reverse attitude from that intended, but there are definitely marks for artisitic impression:

Likes	Dislikes
'That's the one I'll be doing something with. It was a nice pamphlet ... I'm holding on to it.'	'It's too many bits of paper. I could guarantee that I would lose one of these bits of paper and then I'd end up not ordering, even if I was interested.'
	'You want just one sheet giving the information, or something in a booklet that stays together ... Leaflets within leaflets – it's so fiddly.'
	'Junk mail is when you open it and five or six bits fall out.'

Source: Consumer Creative Benchmarks, Direct Mail Information Service, 1995

■ *Do response devices influence the success of the mailing?*

It appears to be crucial to minimise the effort – and cost – of responding.

Likes	Dislikes
'The one thing I do like is the SAE with the Freepost on there.'	'I hate stuff where they send you things through the post and you've to got pay the postage.'
'A pre-printed reply address is a positive – it saves you writing it on, and its more professional than a label.'	'If they expect you to put a stamp on it it's a complete no-no. It's got to be Freepost.'
'A freephone line is good to have.'	'I don't like being pressured. I personally would never respond to an 0800 number, but I might write.'

Source: Consumer Creative Benchmarks, Direct Mail Information Service, 1995

■ *What information should companies provide?*

Special deals and discounts are the most important elements of direct mail. Consumers like to be given product information, especially about food and drink brands. This tends to be more important than price details.

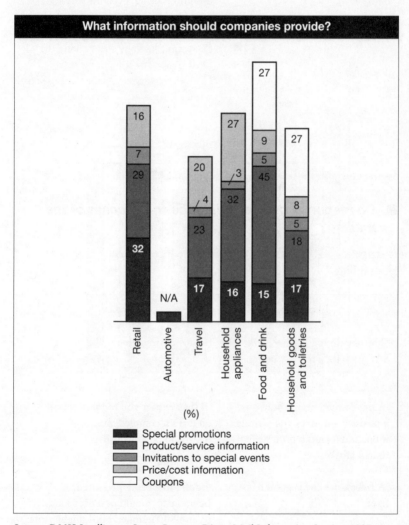

What information should companies provide?

Retail: Special promotions 32, Invitations to special events 29, Price/cost information 7, Coupons 16

Automotive: N/A

Travel: Special promotions 17, Product/service information 23, Invitations to special events 4, Price/cost information 20

Household appliances: Special promotions 16, Product/service information 32, Invitations to special events 3, Price/cost information 27

Food and drink: Special promotions 15, Product/service information 45, Invitations to special events 5, Price/cost information 9, Coupons 27

Household goods and toiletries: Special promotions 17, Product/service information 18, Invitations to special events 5, Price/cost information 8, Coupons 27

(%)

■ Special promotions
Product/service information
Invitations to special events
Price/cost information
□ Coupons

Source: DMIS Intelligence Sector Reports, Direct Mail Information Service, 1997

■ *Do companies provide enough information?*

Sectors which have been using direct mail consistently (like cars and shops) seem to be meeting the need for information. Sectors new to the medium (like household goods and toiletries) are not always providing sufficient information.

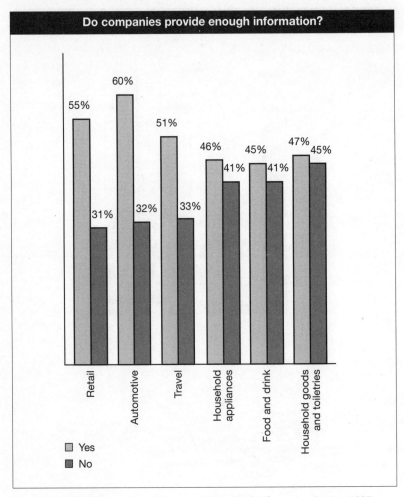

Source: DMIS Intelligence Sector Reports, Direct Mail Information Service, 1997

■ Does direct mail make you more likely to buy from a company?

Direct mail's influence on likelihood to purchase varies between sectors from one quarter to one third. It has the strongest influence in the automotive industry.

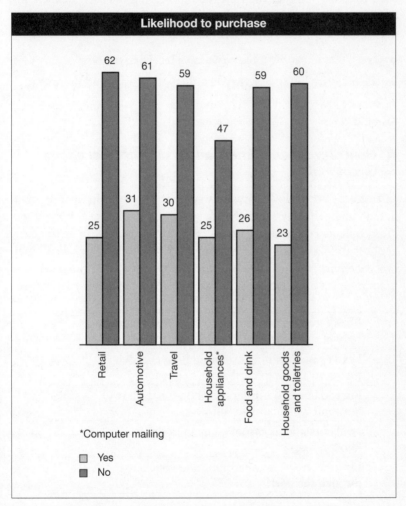

Likelihood to purchase

*Computer mailing

☐ Yes
■ No

Source: DMIS Intelligence Sector Reports, Direct Mail Information Service, 1997

Attitudes to direct mail

■ *How do your customers and prospects feel about receiving mail?*

If you're thinking about communicating with consumers by post, you need to know whether their attitude to hearing the thud of the mail landing on the doormat is a positive or a negative one. The news is good:

- Over 70% of people look forward to receiving the post.
- The majority know exactly when the post arrives, and more than 60% look at it straight away.

Source: Millennium Post, The Henley Centre, 1995

■ *How do your customers and prospects feel about direct mail?*

Just because people look forward to getting a letter from their mum, it doesn't automatically mean that they want to get letters from you. So are people as enthusiastic about letters from companies as they are about mail in general? Or are your letters seen as the 'junk mail' that everyone purports to dislike so much? There is a wide range of attitudes to direct mail, but most people will at least open your letters:

I like receiving offers through the post for goods I might otherwise not know about	51%
I can't resist opening everything but I quickly throw away anything that isn't relevant	79%
I'm too busy, so I order mail into what I'll read now and what can wait till later	23%
I only open letters from companies that I know/recognise	23%
I love receiving competitions and vouchers through the post	31%

Source: Millennium Post, The Henley Centre, 1995

■ *Is your mailshot going to irritate your prospects?*

You may want your message to reach your prospects, but there's no point mailing them if you're just going to irritate them. Their attitude to your company will become more negative than it was before.

You can make an educated guess about which prospects are likely to find your approaches unwelcome if you have detailed information on your database and use clearly targeted mailing lists. The more responsive they have been in the past – either to you or to other companies – the less likely it is that they will be irritated by your mailshot. But in any case, people's attitudes seem to be changing, and most consumers are less inclined to be irritated by direct mail than they were a few years ago.

DIRECT MARKETING

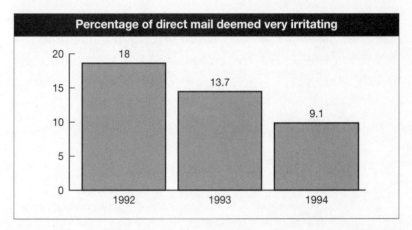

Percentage of direct mail deemed very irritating

Source: European Society for Opinion and Marketing Research (ESOMAR). This material was first presented at the ESOMAR seminar *Advertising, Sponsorship and Promotions: Understanding and Measuring the Effectiveness of Commercial Communication*, Madrid (Spain) March 1995.

■ *What are the most common complaints about direct mail?*

Any direct mail you send out has to comply with certain pieces of legislation, such as the British Code of Advertising Practice, and the British Code of Sales Promotion Practice. If you send out a mailshot that is misleading or appears to make unreasonable claims, people are likely to complain or report you for it, so make sure you follow the rules. The problems, complaints and queries that consumers raise fall into several clear categories.

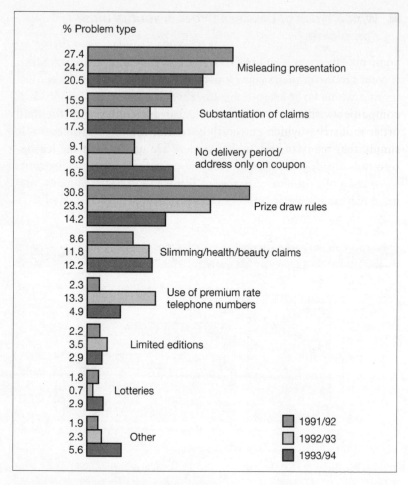

% Problem type

Value	Problem type
27.4 / 24.2 / 20.5	Misleading presentation
15.9 / 12.0 / 17.3	Substantiation of claims
9.1 / 8.9 / 16.5	No delivery period/address only on coupon
30.8 / 23.3 / 14.2	Prize draw rules
8.6 / 11.8 / 12.2	Slimming/health/beauty claims
2.3 / 13.3 / 4.9	Use of premium rate telephone numbers
2.2 / 3.5 / 2.9	Limited editions
1.8 / 0.7 / 2.9	Lotteries
1.9 / 2.3 / 5.6	Other

■ 1991/92
☐ 1992/93
■ 1993/94

Source: Direct Mail Services Standards Board

- The increase in unsubstantiated claims has largely been due to earnings claims in business opportunity schemes and spurious comparisons.

- Problems with the use of premium rate telephone numbers in direct mail have decreased since the device is increasingly used for additional information only, rather than for promotional purposes.

■ Which types of direct mail generate the most complaints?

Some industries seem to break the rules more often than others when it comes to direct mail. This clearly does the reputation of the industry as a whole no good, and therefore reflects badly on the individual companies within it. One of the biggest difficulties with the mail order industry – which currently generates the most problems – is simply that many of the smaller traders are unaware of the legislation, particularly the aspects relating to delivery times. This table shows how the problems are spread across the various industries that use direct mail (the data are for 1993/4).

Business-to-business	5.9%
Charities	2.7%
Clothing	2.9%
Cosmetics/Pharmaceuticals	4.3%
Financial	10.4%
Mail Order	20.2%
Leisure	2.9%
Publishing/Broadcasting	12.2%
Travel	3.5%
Public Utilities	2.1%

Source: Direct Mail Services Standards Board

■ How are your customers influenced by direct mail?

The role direct mail has in informing customers is clear from the way they are influenced by it. Getting general information is the most widely noted impact of mailshots in most sectors. Mailings for retail and household goods and toiletries have the strongest influence on achieving product purchase.

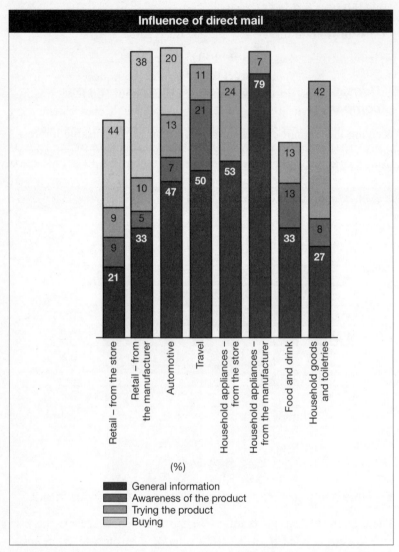

Influence of direct mail

Legend:
- General information
- Awareness of the product
- Trying the product
- Buying

(%)

Source: DMIS Intelligence Sector Reports, Direct Mail Information Service, 1997

What does direct mail say about you?

■ *Are you honest?*

Direct mail presents a certain image that unaddressed mail doesn't. It sends a different message to your prospects.

- Direct mail is considered three times as honest as unaddressed mail according to one survey.

Source: Direct Mail Information Service

■ *Does direct mail give a good impression of your company?*

Receiving direct mail creates an overwhelmingly favourable impression on consumers in most sectors. Yet in the retail sector, it creates a high level of hostility.

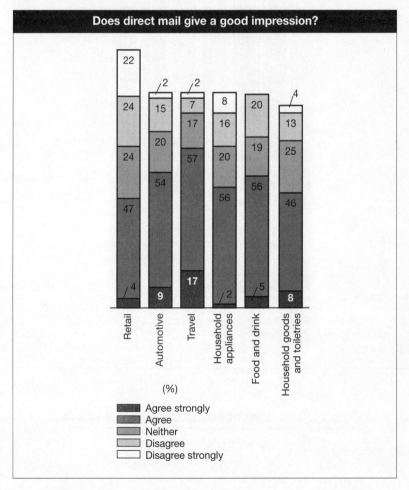

Does direct mail give a good impression?

Source: DMIS Intelligence Sector Reports, Direct Mail Information Service, 1997

DIRECT MARKETING

■ Does responding to direct mail affect your customer's attitude to the company?

As well as achieving a response or sale, it would appear that direct mail lifts brand loyalty. Once a consumer has bought an item as a result of direct mail, their loyalty to the company which mailed them jumps significantly.

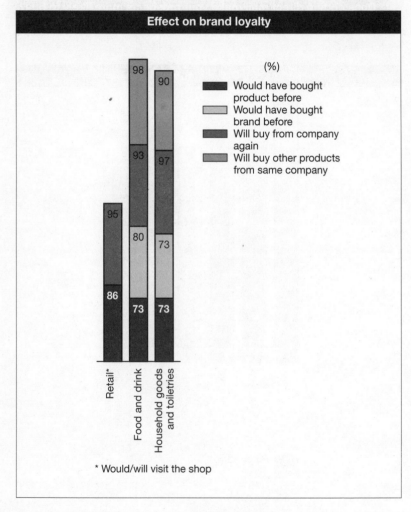

Effect on brand loyalty

(%)

- Would have bought product before
- Would have bought brand before
- Will buy from company again
- Will buy other products from same company

Retail*: 86, 95

Food and drink: 73, 80, 93, 98

Household goods and toiletries: 73, 73, 97, 90

* Would/will visit the shop

Source: DMIS Intelligence Sector Reports, Direct Mail Information Service, 1997

DIRECT MARKETING

■ *Does getting direct mail make your prospects more likely to buy from you?*

Consumers in most sectors are more likely to buy from a company which mails them. If you are marketing automotive products, be careful – in this sector direct mail seems to have a negative affect.

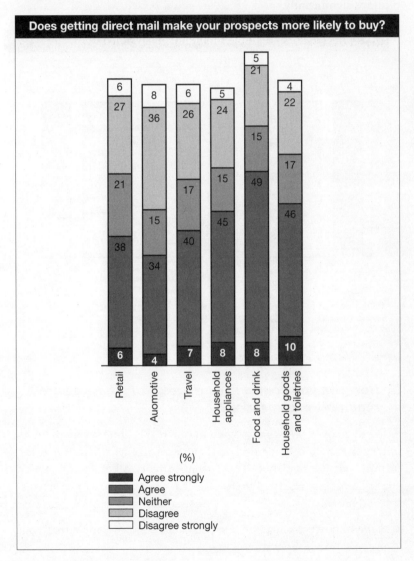

Does getting direct mail make your prospects more likely to buy?

Source: DMIS Intelligence Sector Reports, Direct Mail Information Service, 1997

■ *How important to your company image do you think the practical factors are?*

Direct mail sends out very strong messages about your company that reach people inside their own homes. So it is crucial that you make sure you are putting across exactly the image that you want to. For example, if you want to appear efficient, you'd better not get the address wrong. The following chart shows how important your prospects think these practical factors are to their image of your company.

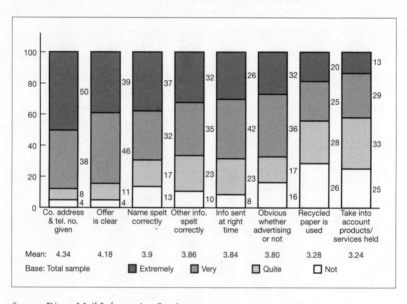

Source: Direct Mail Information Service

■ *How can you convince your prospects that you are a reputable organisation?*

A lot of people will think twice about responding to a company unless they feel confident that they can trust it to live up to the promises of the mailshot. There seem to be two key factors which convey most strongly the impression that your company is trustworthy and reliable:

- A well-known company name persuades 85% of people that your organisation is reputable.

● A return address printed on the envelope reassures 47% of people.

Source: Direct Mail Information Service

The method of response you provide, such as a Freefone number or a business reply envelope, also gives out strong messages about how reputable your organisation is. This is dealt with later in this chapter, on pages 54–74.

Who gets direct mail?

■ First of all, who sends direct mail?

And do they know something you don't? Presumably these types of businesses send direct mail because they find it an effective way to market their goods and services. It's useful to see which industries generate the most consumer direct mail. This indicates whom it works best for, and gives clues as to whose mailpack is likely to land on your prospects' doormats next to yours.

Industry	Percentage of mail order volume
Mail order	18.0
Insurance	10.0
Credit card	4.6
Bank/Girobank	8.2
Building society	2.5
Retailers	7.9
Magazines	2.6
Estate agent	0.6
Manufacturer	6.5
Book club	4.0
Charity	7.2
Gas/electricity board	3.2
Film co.	0.7
Others	24.0
TOTAL	100.0

Source: Direct Mail Information Service

■ *What type of people get the most direct mail?*

People who receive the most direct mail presumably do so because advertisers have found them to be in the most responsive categories. On the other hand, you're competing with more mailings from other organisations when you mail these groups of people. Your own product or service, and your past experience or test mailshots, should tell you which of these opposite factors works best for you.

This chart categorises consumers by sex and by social grade, and indicates what percentage of all the post landing on their doormat is direct mail.

Consumers	Percentage share of letterbox
Total	29
Sex	
Men	28
Women	30
Social Grade	
AB	32
C1	28
C2	26
DE	25

Source: Direct Mail Information Service

■ *How many other pieces of direct mail are you competing with?*

Direct mail may make up a larger percentage of one person's total mail than someone else's, but what about the number of pieces of direct mail they receive? For example, direct mail makes up 2% more of women's mail than of men's, but they both receive the same number of pieces. It's just that women receive slightly fewer other items of mail. So how many individual items of direct mail do these categories of people receive each week?

Consumers	Items of direct mail per week
All	2.0
Sex	
Men	2.2
Women	2.8
Social Grade	
AB	3.3
C1	2.5
C2	1.0
DE	1.3

Source: Direct Mail Trends Survey, Direct Mail Information Service, 1995

■ *What sort of direct mail do consumers want?*

You don't want to waste your time and money by sending people mailpacks they don't want. But 12.7% of consumer direct mail is requested, and it might help to know which kind of products and services people most often ask for direct mail information about. It's a good indication of the sort of products that are suited to direct mail.

Type of product	Percentage requested
Mail order	9.6
Insurance	8.1
Credit card	4.3
Bank/Girobank	8.8
Building society	8.9
Retailers	12.4
Magazines	19.0
Estate agent	70.0
Manufacturer	13.2
Book club	17.0
Charity	7.0
Gas/electricity board	8.9
Film co.	12.0
Others	14.1

Source: Direct Mail Information Service

Getting your prospects to open the envelope

■ How do consumers treat direct mail?

Will your prospects and customers open the envelope, and, if so, when? Some people open and read their direct mail immediately, while others never open it at all. The time they read the mailshot could affect the mood in which they read it, or whether they read it hurriedly or at leisure. These factors, in turn, can affect how much they take in and whether or not they respond.

Open and read immediately	37%
Open immediately and read later that day	14%
Open immediately and read later	9%
Open and read later in the day	6%
Open and read sometime afterwards	11%
Open but don't read	11%
Don't open	11%
None	2%

Source: Direct Mail Information Service

■ *What persuades people to open the letters they receive from you?*

The Henley Centre used facsimile versions of five different envelopes to find out how people decide which to open first.

- Over 80% would open either of two 'personal' looking envelopes first – usually a large white envelope, followed by a manilla one.

- The three most obviously promotional envelopes were opened first by only a few people.

- A prize draw envelope was almost always opened last.

The chart below shows the reasons that people gave (without being prompted) for opening individual envelopes first and last.

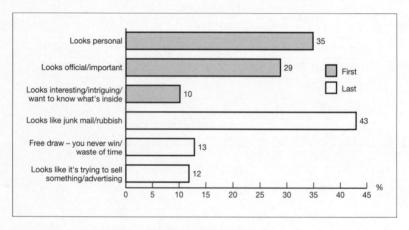

Source: The Millennium Post, The Henley Centre, 1995

■ *Are consumers more likely to open the envelope if they know it's from you?*

This depends very much on whether or not they can tell that it contains advertising material. The growth in relationship marketing – building an individual relationship with your customers – has led to more non-advertising mailshots, so your customers may not be able to guess the contents of the envelope without opening it.

If your mailshot to customers who know you is not recognisable as advertising, it is more likely to be opened than direct mail from companies they have never heard of. On the other hand, if they can tell that it's advertising they are *less* likely to open it than they would be if they hadn't heard of you. The following table shows the results of a survey in which respondents were asked how they responded to the last item of direct mail they received.

Response	Opened	Read
Knew who sent item, knew it was advertising	77%	62%
Knew who sent item, did not know it was advertising	94%	80%
Did not know who sent item, knew it was advertising	81%	60%
Did not know who sent item, did not know it was advertising	90%	77%

Source: Direct Mail Information Service, 1993

■ *Which type of people are most likely to open and read your mailshot?*

There are two different questions here, since opening and reading mail don't necessarily go together. Women, for example, are more likely to open direct mail, but less likely to read it.

Consumers	Opened	Read
All	78%	64%
Sex		
Men	76%	60%
Women	81%	67%
Social Grade		
AB		68%
C1		63%
C2		57%
DE		69%

Source: Direct Mail Trends Survey, Direct Mail Information Service, 1995

■ *How many people will keep your direct mail for future reference?*

A lot of people don't want your product at the time your mailshot arrives, but they may be aware of a possible need for it later, so they hang on to the information for future reference. The degree to which this happens varies from one sector to the next, but it is almost certainly happening several times for every customer who orders from you, as the chart shows.

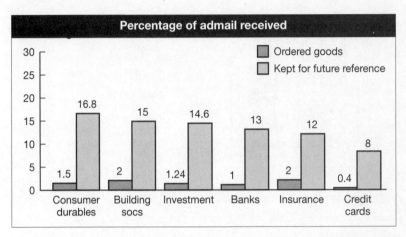

Source: European Society for Opinion and Marketing Research (ESOMAR). This material was first presented at the ESOMAR seminar *Advertising, Sponsorship and Promotions: Understanding and Measuring the Effectiveness of Commercial Communication,* Madrid (Spain), March 1995.

■ *Do people pass on direct mail?*

Generally speaking, direct mail is used to target individuals. You might think that each person you mail will either respond or not respond. But your mailshot is in fact frequently passed on to someone else.

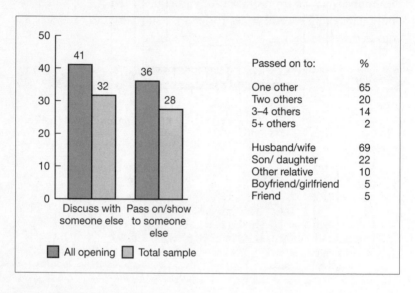

Passed on to:	%
One other	65
Two others	20
3–4 others	14
5+ others	2
Husband/wife	69
Son/ daughter	22
Other relative	10
Boyfriend/girlfriend	5
Friend	5

Source: Direct Mail Information Service

Response options

■ *What type of direct mail would influence you?*

Getting a good deal matters most to people who receive direct mail. Immediate discounts such as coupons have the greatest influence. All sectors can influence purchase through mailings about special offers.

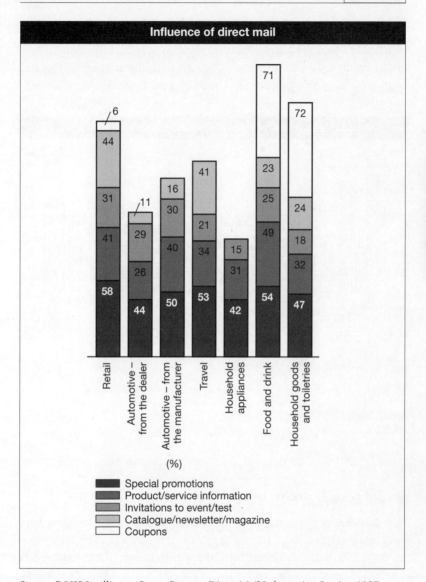

Source: DMIS Intelligence Sector Reports, Direct Mail Information Service, 1997

■ *How much direct mail is wasted?*

Consumers appear to be keen to receive information. Fewer than one in ten consumers say that they have not opened or read any of the items they have received.

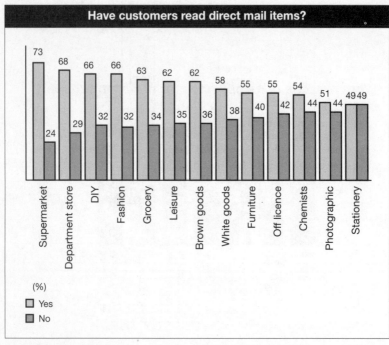

Have customers read direct mail items?

Supermarket: 73 / 24
Department store: 68 / 29
DIY: 66 / 32
Fashion: 66 / 32
Grocery: 63 / 34
Leisure: 62 / 35
Brown goods: 62 / 36
White goods: 58 / 38
Furniture: 55 / 40
Off licence: 55 / 42
Chemists: 54 / 44
Photographic: 51 / 44
Stationery: 49 / 49

(%)
☐ Yes
☐ No

Source: DMIS Intelligence Sector Reports, Direct Mail Information Service, 1997

■ *Do people prefer to respond by phone or by post?*

It seems that people still prefer to use the post, at least for their first response, despite the growing range of free and low cost telephone options available. It seems to make a difference what their social grade is, however. The higher the grade, the more likely they are to respond by phone. The following chart shows the percentage of people preferring to make their first reply by post.

Social group	Percentage
A1	62
AB	54
C1	62
C2	64
DE	69

Source: Direct Mail Information Service

■ *What reasons do people give for preferring to reply by post?*

Those people who prefer the post seem to feel that it offers greater emotional comfort, security and control. They also tend to consider it cheaper. The majority of people prefer to be given a free option for responding, but there are some who prefer to use a stamp. And one in five people surveyed believe that adding a stamp to a Freepost or Business Reply envelope 'speeds it up'.

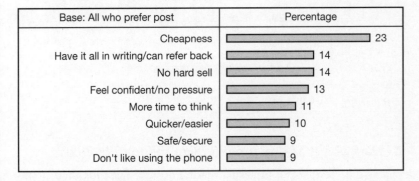

Base: All who prefer post	Percentage
Cheapness	23
Have it all in writing/can refer back	14
No hard sell	14
Feel confident/no pressure	13
More time to think	11
Quicker/easier	10
Safe/secure	9
Don't like using the phone	9

Source: Direct Mail Information Service

■ *What are the most effective response options?*

The size of response that you get to a direct mailshot can be strongly influenced by the options that you offer for responding. Interestingly, this survey showed that companies that asked their customers or prospects to reply only by post achieved a higher response rate than those which offered a choice of responding by either post or phone.

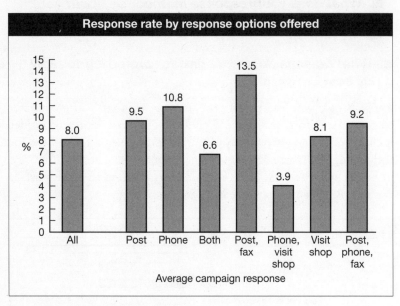

Source: Direct Mail Information Service

■ *How about asking prospects to respond by fax?*

The last chart also showed what happens when you invite people to respond by fax. Clearly, this is only an option if they are likely to have a fax machine. When this is the case, however, you could go one step further and enclose a fax response sheet. This should include tick boxes with options such as 'please send me further information' or 'please contact me to arrange an appointment'.

● According to one piece of research, this can increase your response rate by 50%.

Source: John Fenton Training International plc

■ *What does your response method say about you?*

Consumers will judge you by the type of response method you offer them. Enclosing a first class Business Reply sends out a very different message from an invitation to phone a standard telephone number. This chart shows how many people agree that certain response methods give the impression that the company concerned is bona fide, and that its products or services are good quality.

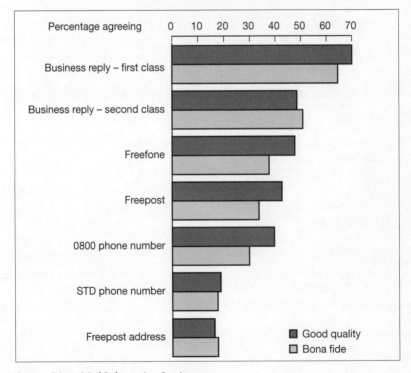

Source: Direct Mail Information Service

Response rates

■ *What type of direct mail do consumers respond to?*

Some people just don't respond to direct mail. For example, only 31% responded to catalogues. But of those who do, it's useful to know what type of mailing they are most likely to respond to.

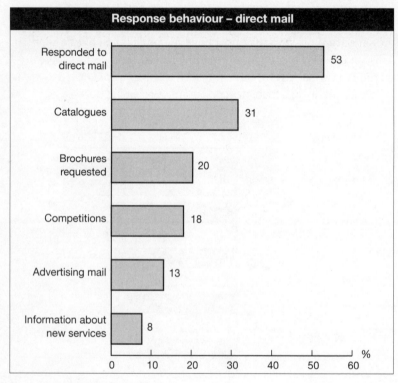

Response behaviour – direct mail

Responded to direct mail	53
Catalogues	31
Brochures requested	20
Competitions	18
Advertising mail	13
Information about new services	8

Source: Direct Mail Information Service

■ *How often do consumers respond to direct mail?*

Half of consumers respond only once or twice a year. We've already seen that the average number of items of direct mail is 1.7 a week, which is 88.4 a year. So it must take a significant offer to persuade these people to respond. We've also seen that direct mail is frequently passed on to someone else – usually someone in the household – so to get the full picture, you also need to know how many times these people will respond.

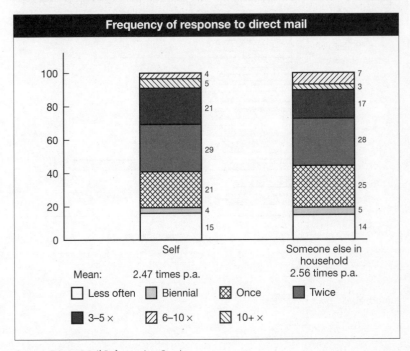

Source: Direct Mail Information Service

■ *How does the response rate vary according to the type of response you want?*

You would expect the response rate to a questionnaire to differ from the response rate to an order form. But by how much? This chart shows the average response rates to a number of campaigns, according to the type of response asked for.

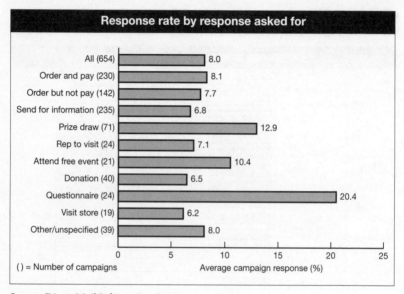

Response rate by response asked for

Response asked for	Average campaign response (%)
All (654)	8.0
Order and pay (230)	8.1
Order but not pay (142)	7.7
Send for information (235)	6.8
Prize draw (71)	12.9
Rep to visit (24)	7.1
Attend free event (21)	10.4
Donation (40)	6.5
Questionnaire (24)	20.4
Visit store (19)	6.2
Other/unspecified (39)	8.0

( ) = Number of campaigns   Average campaign response (%)

Source: Direct Mail Information Service

■ *Which industries get the best response?*

Clearly, the response level you can expect to a direct mail campaign is going to be affected by the type of industry you are in. So, in order to measure your success, it would help to know what the average response rate for your industry is. The following chart shows precisely that, for over 20 sectors.

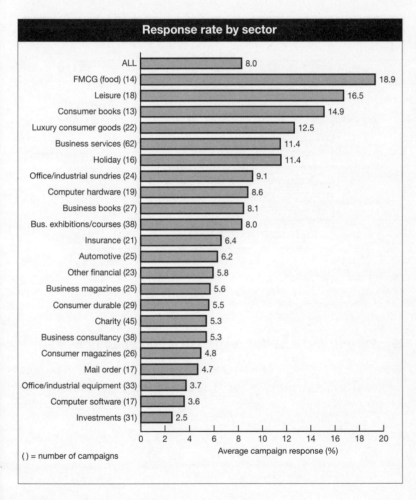

Response rate by sector

Sector	Average campaign response (%)
ALL	8.0
FMCG (food) (14)	18.9
Leisure (18)	16.5
Consumer books (13)	14.9
Luxury consumer goods (22)	12.5
Business services (62)	11.4
Holiday (16)	11.4
Office/industrial sundries (24)	9.1
Computer hardware (19)	8.6
Business books (27)	8.1
Bus. exhibitions/courses (38)	8.0
Insurance (21)	6.4
Automotive (25)	6.2
Other financial (23)	5.8
Business magazines (25)	5.6
Consumer durable (29)	5.5
Charity (45)	5.3
Business consultancy (38)	5.3
Consumer magazines (26)	4.8
Mail order (17)	4.7
Office/industrial equipment (33)	3.7
Computer software (17)	3.6
Investments (31)	2.5

( ) = number of campaigns

Source: Direct Mail Information Service

DIRECT MARKETING

■ *Does the size of the mailing affect the response rate?*

You might well think that the number of people you mail couldn't possibly affect the rate of response. But in fact, smaller mailings tend to be better targeted. As a result, they are likely to achieve a higher level of response. Of course, the biggest mailings, while perhaps drawing a lower percentage response, can still pull huge volumes.

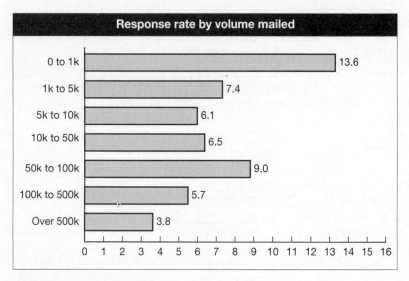

Source: Direct Mail Information Service

■ *Will you get a better response if you spend more?*

In general, the amount of money you spend on creating each mailing pack will influence the response. The cheaper the pack, the lower the response. Of course, the value of each response will tell you whether it's worth spending the extra or not.

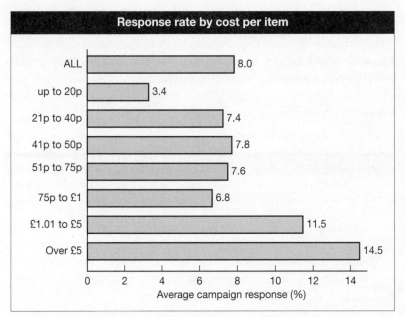

Source: Direct Mail Information Service

■ *What type of responses do people make to direct mail?*

There are lots of reasons to reply to a mailshot, from asking for more information to placing an order. When you send out a mailshot, do you know how many enquiries you expect, how many orders, and so on? Here's an indication of the main purpose of responses to direct mail.

To buy goods	42%
To send for information	24%
To send for goods on approval	10%
To make an enquiry	10%
To enter a prize draw	8%
To order a service	5%
To make a donation	1%

Source: Direct Mail Information Service

■ *How much can you influence the response rate by adapting the mailshot?*

The most startling piece of evidence in answer to this question comes from the direct marketing guru Drayton Bird. He says:

> *If you take all the factors that go into a direct marketing programme, remarkable differences can emerge, as I discovered a few years ago when we were launching a new financial product. We tested 12 different mailing lists, three possible purchase prices, two different ways of paying, two different times of the year, and several creative elements. The most profitable test cell performed 58 times better than the least – a result calculated to give anyone interested in return on investment a warm feeling indeed.*

To be more specific, here is the difference that each of these factors individually can make to your response rate, but do remember that these separate improvements cannibalise each other. Two tests giving a 20% improvement each will not, combined, produce 40%. It may be 30% or less.

Factor	Difference between best and worst
Mailing list	× 6.0
Offer	× 3.0
Timing	× 2.0
Creative	× 1.35
Response mechanics	× 1.2

Source: The Drayton Bird Partnership

Business-to-business

■ *How many managers open their own mail?*

You've put a lot of effort into creating a mailshot that grabs the prospect's attention. But are your prospects actually going to open, or even see, your material? Most managers open their own post, but a significant number have a 'filterer' who opens and sorts their mail for them. But does this mean that your attempts to attract the prospect have been foiled, or merely delayed by a few minutes?

- Fewer managers have filterers now than did a couple of years ago: one quarter now compared to 30% in 1993.

- This cutback has been deepest in medium-sized companies, with 50 to 99 staff.

- Research by DMIS showed that, in general, the filterer's role is not to block out items of mail, but simply to structure the post according to the importance of its contents.

Source: Direct Mail Information Service

■ How useful do managers consider direct mail to be?

The average manager receives 15 items of direct mail a week at work. If some of them are coming from you, it may help if managers have a positive attitude towards it. So do they think it's useful? 43% of managers reckon it is.

Very useful	9%
Quite useful	34%
Indifferent	14%
Not very useful	23%
Not at all useful	14%
Question not answered	4%

Source: Direct Mail Information Service

It's worth adding that this survey found that non-managerial professionals such as doctors, lawyers and architects find direct mail particularly useful as a way of finding out about products and services that might not be readily available from other sources.

■ What attitudes do business people have to direct mail?

Apart from the question of usefulness, what other views do business people have about direct mail? The following research findings include usefulness among a group of other factors about which business people were asked. The findings suggest that well produced direct mail, at least, is more positively regarded than it was a few years ago. Incidentally, the answers shown in this table are specifically from managers who open their own post, rather than having it filtered by a secretary or PA.

Attitude	Percentage of managers	
	1991	1994
Waste of time	35	27
Other general negative comment	25	19
Waste of material	20	16
Useful source of information for work	19	13
Just part of the working day	14	11
OK/good as long as done well	8	21
A general positive comment	10	11
Other	10	18
Question not answered	1	1

Source: Direct Mail Information Service

■ How do business people feel about inaccuracies in the address of their direct mail?

Is your mailing list as accurate as it should be? It's even more important with business-to-business mailings than with consumers, because a relatively minor error could prevent the mailshot ever reaching its target. But quite apart from that, it makes a bad impression on the business people you are mailing.

● An average of one in three business mailings contains some form of error in the address.

● 78% of business people think that an inaccurate address reflects badly on the company that sent the mailshot.

Source: Direct Mail Information Service

■ *How do business people feel about duplicate direct mail?*

It creates a very bad impression of your organisation if you duplicate business names and addresses on your mailing list.

● 72% of business people agree that duplicate mail 'annoys them intensely'.

Source: Direct Mail Information Service

■ *How do business people treat direct mail?*

Is your mailshot going to be opened? If it's not appropriate for the person you sent it to, will they bother to pass it on to anyone else? The following chart shows how business people treat the direct mail they receive.

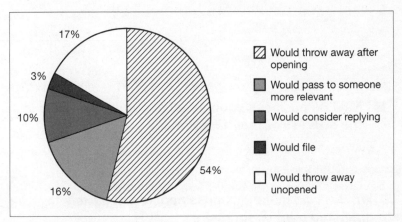

17%

3%

10%

16%

54%

☒ Would throw away after opening

▨ Would pass to someone more relevant

■ Would consider replying

■ Would file

□ Would throw away unopened

Source: Direct Mail Information Service

■ *What do business people do with the direct mail that they don't open?*

Just over one in six mailpacks are left unopened; more than the figure three years ago. If your prospect doesn't even open your mail, the chances are it's because they 'can see what it is from the outside' (this is the explanation in just over half of cases). Another quarter will tell you that it's because it is either a duplicate or an irrelevant item.

69

But if the prospect doesn't open it, is that the end of your mail-pack, or does it have some hope of a last-minute reprieve? The following table shows that there's still a chance that it might be passed on to someone else. Failing that, a few of your mailpacks may finally make it back home, where you can use them to purge your database. This table lists answers from managers, and from people who filter the post for their manager.

Action taken with unopened mail						
Base: Total items left unopened	1991			1994		
	All business managers	Filterers	Total sample	All business managers	Filterers	Total sample
Throw away	69%	59%	65%	76%	42%	70%
Pass to business manager	–	11%	4%	–	34%	5%
Look at and throw away	–	–	–	9%	–	7%
Pass to more relevant/ appropriate person	22%	28%	24%	11%	15%	12%
Return to sender/PO	8%	2%	6%	4%	10%	5%

Source: Direct Mail Information Service

■ *What would make business people more likely to open and read direct mail?*

The best place to get this information is straight from the horse's mouth. And that's exactly what the DMIS did. They asked business managers, and the people who filter their mail for them (where this applied), how they would ensure that business direct mail was opened and read.

Presentation factors seemed to be the strongest; respondents said they would be most likely to open a thick package with a hand-written address. The next most likely to be opened was an item with a postage stamp and a typed address. The reason seemed to be, typically, that respondents would assume that not so many had been sent out, which gives a particular item a touch of class.

Action	Business managers		Filterers
	Without filterer	With filterer	
Accuracy			
Personalise the mail	23	26	13
Correct name (spelt)	21	13	22
Correct address	18	15	17
Presentation			
Make envelope interesting but not gaudy etc.	24	22	26
Must appear to have value/ status/significance	13	11	13
Other presentation issues	39	35	35
Relevance			
Ensure it goes to right person	14	11	11
Phone/contact/ensure relevance/interest	15	17	7
Free gift/discount/offer	13	11	4

Source: Direct Mail Information Service

■ *Why do business people respond to direct mail?*

Among managers without a filterer, as many as 5% of the items they receive might get a response. This may not be immediate, and it may be from someone else in the organisation. But it means that you start with a 1 in 20 chance that yours will be one of the items that gets a response. It might help to bump up the likelihood of your prospects responding to something better than 1 in 20, but to do that, you need to know what sort of items managers are most likely to respond to. The following research questioned business managers who have responded, or would consider responding, to direct mail about their reasons for doing so.

It has to be relevant to the business	28%
Incentive or discount/offer/'freebies'	14%
Invitation to open day/seminar	3%
To prepare prices/service in future policy	2%
Other	2%
Don't know/not responded	59%

Source: Direct Mail Information Service

■ How often do business people respond to direct mail?

When you're sending out your mailpack, it might help to know what you're up against. Are you asking managers, by responding, to do something they do habitually? Or are you asking them to venture into what is a completely new type of behaviour? The following table shows you when the managers in this survey last responded to business direct mail.

Within last month	33%
Within last 6 months	21%
Within last year	5%
Longer ago	1%
Never	40%
Don't know	–

Source: Direct Mail Information Service

■ How do business people respond to direct mail?

Presumably your mailpack will invite your prospects to respond to you. But what method will you ask them to use? That rather depends on how you think they will want to respond. So what method do business people prefer to use? The following chart shows how the business managers surveyed responded on the most recent occasion that they replied to a piece of direct mail.

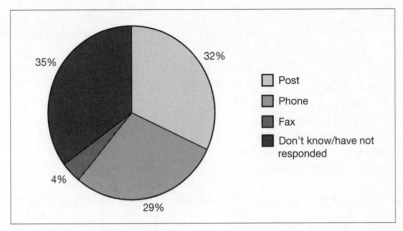

Source: Direct Mail Information Service

DIRECT MARKETING

■ How about asking prospects to respond by fax?

Offering people the option of responding by fax can improve your response rates considerably. (If this doesn't seem to tally with the earlier table, remember that the previous table didn't indicate which options were available to the respondents.) Test this approach, since it will work better for some businesses than others. In any case, this is likely to work best if you enclose a fax response sheet. This should include tick boxes with options such as 'please send me further information' or 'please contact me to arrange an appointment'.

- According to one piece of research, this can increase your response rate by 50%.

Source: John Fenton Training International plc

■ Are some kinds of direct mail more likely to interest business people than others?

The response you get from managers to your mailshots will depend a good deal on what line of business you're in. Managers are far more likely to open mail from some types of company than others. Here's a guide to how they respond to a selection of over a dozen company types that commonly target managers through direct mail.

Company types	Look at/ throw away	Pass on	File	Consider responding	No experience/ question not answered
Banks	51	16	8	1	24
Insurance	58	14	4	4	21
Transport (people)	49	16	19	-	18
Transport (goods)	41	19	18	3	20
Hotels/catering	45	20	16	1	18
Conferences/seminars	43	18	23	3	13
Relevant services/ products	18	18	48	9	7
Telecoms/IT	50	23	16	1	9
Mail order (consumer)	64	10	4	2	20
Mail order (office)	47	21	18	4	12
Charities	38	17	5	18	20
Book clubs	52	4	5	-	39
Credit card	55	6	3	-	36

Source: Direct Mail Information Service

Testing

■ *What should you test?*

If you never test your mailshots, you'll never know if you could have got a better response. Send out mailshots that differ in some way and then compare the response. Only change one factor each time, or you won't know which one made the difference. The most common factors to test for are:

- Product variations
- Price and discounts
- New lists and database selection
- Timing – e.g. months, days of the week, special occasions
- Easier order mechanisms
- Volume of material in fulfilment pack
- Gimmicks

Source: The Drayton Bird Partnership

■ How large a sample should you test?

The higher the response you expect, the smaller the numbers you need for a valid test result. Suppose you want 500 responses for a test. If you expect a 5% response rate, you'll need to mail a test of 10,000. But if you expect a 10% response, you'll only need to mail 5,000. You'll need to use probability tables to work out the accuracy of the test but, for example, at a response rate of 2%, 17,000 mailing pieces gives 340 responses. This gives a 95% probability to within 0.25% either way.

Source: The Drayton Bird Partnership

■ When should you test?

If you run a test at a time when there is some external factor at work, your results won't be representative. Be very sceptical of test results that are derived during:

- Dramatic news
- Very good weather
- A peak period in your competitors' activity
- Christmas
- Public holidays

Source: The Drayton Bird Partnership

■ How soon will you know the results of your tests?

It clearly depends on your business, but you can't finalise the plans for your campaign until you get some results to your tests. So you need to know when that will be.

- Results build to a peak, then tail off.
- Failures tail off faster than successes.
- Successes build more, and last longer.

Source: The Drayton Bird Partnership

Learning from mistakes

■ *Where do new direct marketers go wrong most?*

Drayton Bird, of The Drayton Bird Partnership, reckons there are nine ways in which new direct marketers go wrong. They are:

1 **They rush it.** It takes longer than you think – maybe three months – to carry out a mailing from briefing to 'drop'; longer to plan and carry out a complete campaign.

2 **They try to do it on the cheap.** This is not a cheap alternative; it's a different discipline.

3 **They don't pay enough attention to detail.** There are 100 steps in carrying out a direct mail campaign – which gives you 100 chances to screw up.

4 **They ignore brand values.** It's stupid to say one thing in ads and another in direct mail, or to have one look in one and a different one in another.

5 **They are inconsistent.** Don't have one style for the first campaign, then another for the next. For the same reason, stick to one agency unless you have the time and resources to supervise the campaign yourself.

6 **They stop and start.** Think in terms of continuing campaigns which build loyalty.

7 **They ignore the 'back-end'.** Don't send out inadequate material or delay responses to enquiries – this can ruin your efforts.

8 **They don't understand how vital testing is.** So test thoroughly – and read the results carefully, making sure that they are appropriate and accurate.

9 **They don't deal with specialists.** People with sales promotion or advertising backgrounds rarely understand direct marketing. So try and find a specialist.

Source: Drayton Bird, The Drayton Bird Partnership

TELEMARKETING

■ *What is telemarketing?*

Telemarketing is an umbrella term which includes using the telephone for prospecting, selling, handling enquiries and orders, dealing with complaints, and improving customer service. (You will find some aspects of this covered in Chapter 5 as part of customer care.)

Telemarketing calls for an integrated approach to communicating with individual customers by phone, so that any call – incoming or outgoing, a query or a sale – can be dealt with and recorded on the customer's file. Over time, you can build up a detailed and unique file on each and every customer, which will inform and guide the next contact you have with them.

First impressions

■ *How do you make your first impressions count?*

All companies rely on the telephone to maintain contact with customers and suppliers. As the telephone is the first point of contact many customers will have with your company and because first impressions do last, it is important that everybody receives thorough training in telephone customer care.

So how do you maximise the selling potential of that first call? Marcus Child, Director of Training at customer service consultancy Managing the Service Business (MSB) Ltd, reckons training is the answer. He comments:

Telephone training is an issue for everybody in business. Companies should ensure that all employees answer the telephone promptly and politely and return calls in a timely fashion.

Source: Marcus Child, Director of Training, Managing the Service Business (MSB) Ltd

■ Can you improve your telephone manner?

Marcus Child offers ten top tips for improving telephone etiquette:

1 **Phones should be answered within three rings.**

2 **When answering the telephone say** 'good morning/afternoon/evening', give the company name, give your own name, and ask 'how can I help you?'

3 **Know how to transfer calls.**

4 **If unanswered, calls should bounce** to a colleague or administrator with voice mail as the secondary option.

5 **All voice mail boxes should have up-to-date messages** – callers need to have an idea of the timescale in which they can expect a return call. If you are going to be out of the office for more than a couple of days, make sure the message gives the name and number of somebody else who can deal with queries/emergencies and so on in your absence.

6 **Retrieve voice mail messages regularly.** Nothing frustrates a customer more than being ignored. Indeed, 67% of customers who take their business elsewhere do so because nobody has kept in touch with them.

7 **Messages should be returned within one working day,** or alternative arrangements made – perhaps for a colleague to take calls in your absence.

8 **Never ignore messages from people within your own organisation.** Failure to return calls is not only bad manners but conveys an unprofessional image. Moreover, it will create extra work as colleagues look for alternative channels, such as e-mail, to gain your attention. It also fuels office politics and encourages others to copy your slack behaviour, leading to a breakdown in internal communications.

9 **Manage your workload.** Recent research has highlighted how today's executive is bombarded by messages – up to 56 phone calls and 21 voice mail messages alone per day. Do NOT be tempted to use voice mail as a means of dodging calls.

10 **Harness the technology to prioritise your work.** When you are working to a deadline arrange for a colleague to deal with enquiries or take messages; as a last resort leave an explanatory

voice mail. When retrieving voice mail messages, prioritise calls in order of urgency/importance. For non-urgent messages, arrange for a colleague or administrator to return the call.

Source: Marcus Child, Director of Training, Managing the Service Business (MSB) Ltd

Part of the marketing mix

■ How can you use the phone to boost your direct mail response rates?

You can use the telephone in combination with direct mail to try to achieve higher response rates than you would with either medium on its own. The research findings here are guidelines only; obviously the precise response rates you can expect will vary according to your line of business. So you will need to test the method you think you want to use to find out what your own response rate is. The guidelines that follow indicate various ways of combining direct mail with telemarketing, and show the average response rate for each approach.

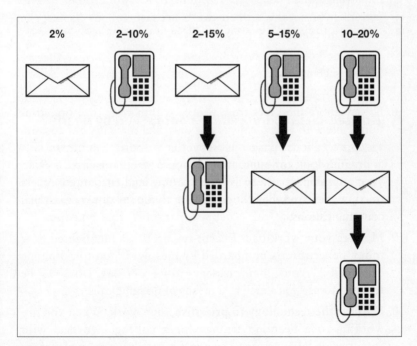

Source: Calcom Associates

It's worth pointing out that the highest response rate may not be the most cost effective for you. Phone calls take time and cost money, and for some companies it is more effective to minimise them or to use direct mail only. Another option that may work for you is to use direct mail for the bulk of your prospects and simply use the direct mail/phone combination for the most promising ones.

■ How often do you need to update your prospect and customer lists?

People move house or change jobs or office location. So to get the maximum response from your marketing campaigns, you need to keep your list up to date. We've already seen that inaccurate contact details put you in danger of failing to reach your customer or prospect. You also run the risk of irritating them considerably, by failing to keep accurate and up-to-date details about them.

Whether you're marketing by direct mail or by telephone, the quickest and most effective way to check your list is by phone. So how often do you need to update your list?

● According to British Telecom, the 'decay rate' of lists often exceeds 20% a year.

Source: British Telecom

■ Do your customers want to contact you by phone?

People like to use the phone for some things more than others, such as complaining, or ordering pizzas. Should you be making it easier for your customers to phone you? The following matrix indicates the proportion of people who like to use the phone for certain functions, and also the frequency with which they carry out these functions.

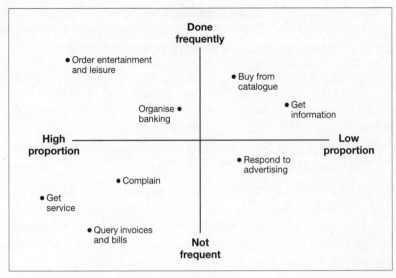

Source: *Telebusiness survey*, The Henley Centre 1994

■ *What reasons do people cite for preferring to respond by phone?*

Slightly under half of consumers choose to use the phone rather than the post to respond to direct mail. Speed is the phone's chief benefit, along with the fact that it's more personal than using the post. The following chart shows why those who chose the phone made that choice:

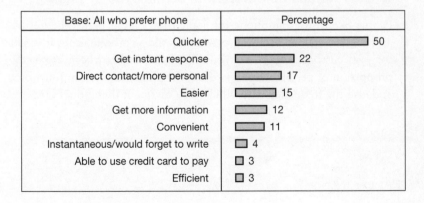

Base: All who prefer phone	Percentage
Quicker	50
Get instant response	22
Direct contact/more personal	17
Easier	15
Get more information	12
Convenient	11
Instantaneous/would forget to write	4
Able to use credit card to pay	3
Efficient	3

Source: Direct Mail Information Service

Call answering

■ *Are all your customers getting through to you?*

Clearly you want every customer to have as easy a time of it as possible when they call you. We all know from personal experience how frustrating it is when we can't get hold of the right person on the phone. Does it really happen as often as we feel it does, or do we just remember the bad experiences? Are you putting your own customers through the same frustrations when they dial your number?

- According to BT figures, three out of every four calls to businesses do not achieve their objective at the first attempt, either because lines are engaged or because the caller can't get through to the right person.

Source: British Telecom

■ *If your customers can't get through first time, will they call back?*

Not surprisingly, it makes a lot of difference what business you're in. But the following findings suggest that whatever business it is, you will lose some callers for good if they can't get through to you. And if you're placing an ad that includes a contact phone number, you'd better be sure that your phone system and staffing levels are well prepared to deal with the response.

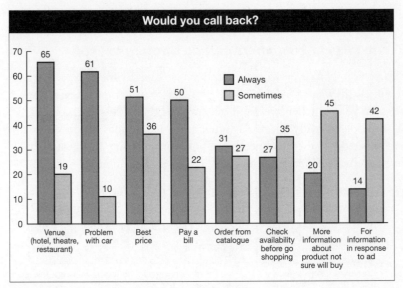

Would you call back?

Source: *Telebusiness Survey*, The Henley Centre 1994

■ *How do your customers feel when you play music down the phone at them?*

How do you feel about it when other organisations do it to you? It is one of the least popular telephone queuing systems as far as the callers are concerned. Yet it is the most commonly used by companies.

If you're stuck with it because you have an out-of-date system, the Henley Centre's research suggests that there is at least anecdotal evidence that you can win back a few brownie points if you select music to suit your target audience's taste.

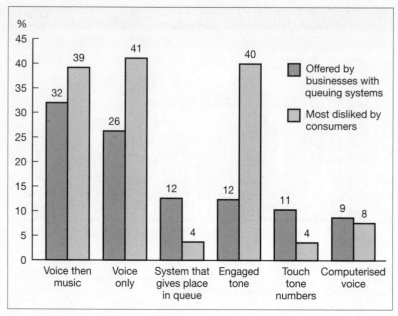

Source: Telebusiness Survey, The Henley Centre 1994

Dealing with people over the phone

■ *What do your customers want from a phone call to your company?*

One of the main reasons that consumers like to use the phone is because it's convenient and quick. So it's hardly surprising that speed and efficiency are top of their list of what makes for a good call. The following chart also shows what other attitudes and responses your customers are looking for when they dial your number.

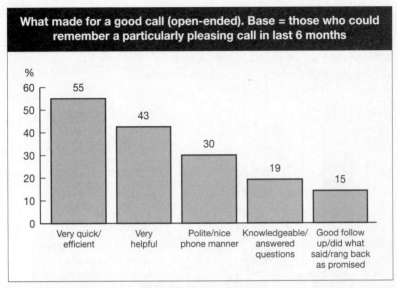

What made for a good call (open-ended). Base = those who could remember a particularly pleasing call in last 6 months

Source: Telebusiness survey, The Henley Centre 1994

■ *What are the components of a good call?*

The Henley Centre identified through its research the 'three Cs' of good call handling – Convenience, Cordiality and Consistency – and has broken each of them down into their component parts. Every one of these factors should be present in every call to your company.

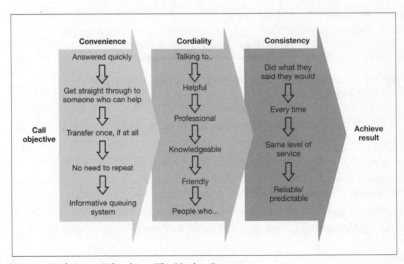

Source: High Street Teleculture, The Henley Centre

DIRECT MARKETING

■ *Does it make much difference if you handle a call badly?*

Yes it does. Just a single badly handled call will deter over two thirds of customers from doing business with you again.

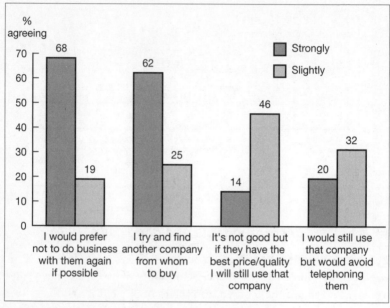

Source: *Telebusiness survey*, The Henley Centre, 1994

Selling over the phone

■ *How likely are people to buy from you over the phone?*

It seems that certain factors have a strong influence on people's willingness to buy over the phone. The most significant of these turn out to be how interested and confident they are in the particular market you are in.

The following chart gives a good indication, for a wide range of products and markets, of the difference that the consumer's confidence and interest will have on the likelihood of their buying by phone.

DIRECT MARKETING

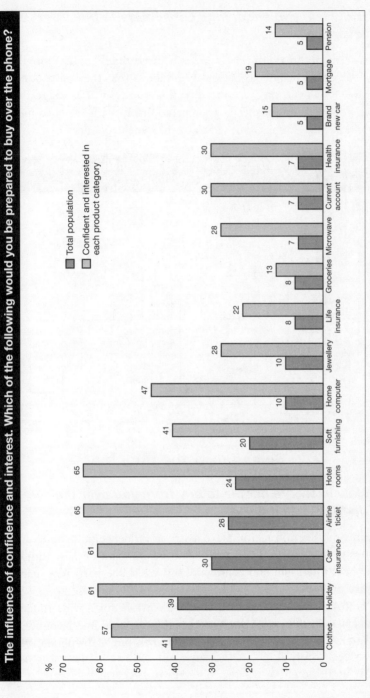

The influence of confidence and interest. Which of the following would you be prepared to buy over the phone?

- Total population
- Confident and interested in each product category

	Total population	Confident and interested
Clothes	57	41
Holiday	61	39
Car insurance	61	30
Airline ticket	65	26
Hotel rooms	65	24
Soft furnishing	41	20
Home computer	47	10
Jewellery	28	10
Life insurance	22	8
Groceries	13	8
Microwave	28	7
Current account	30	7
Health insurance	30	7
Brand new car	15	5
Mortgage	19	5
Pension	14	5

Source: Telebusiness survey, The Henley Centre, 1994

■ How can you encourage consumers to buy from you over the phone?

This seems to be a bit of a catch-22, because the thing that most persuades people to buy from you by phone is that they have done so before. However, the research into this question does suggest that once you have established a good relationship with the customer, it should become far easier to sell to them over the phone.

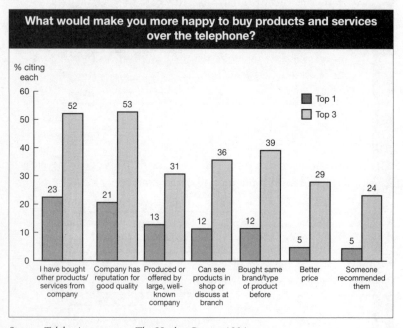

What would make you more happy to buy products and services over the telephone?

Source: Telebusiness survey, The Henley Centre, 1994

■ How do you measure your telephone selling performance?

You – or your sales staff – will make numerous calls that don't get through to the right person, at least not first time. Even when you do get through, the call may not result in an order. It could be a straight 'no', or it could be a step on the way to a possible sale. And then you'll make some calls (one hopes) that will end in a sale. And out of this mixed bag of call types, you need to find some way of measuring how well you're doing. Otherwise you can't tell if performance is going up or down, or whether one type of list earns you better results than another. What you need is a formula for calculating your performance; so here it is.

You need to keep a tally of three things:

---

1 DIALS: count the number of times you dial a phone number and hear a voice at the other end of the line saying 'Good morning'. Even if you get no further than the receptionist, add the call to your score. Only engaged or disconnected tones fail to score.

---

2 C CALLS: score one point every time you get as far as speaking to someone who is in a position to place an order – whether or not they actually do – that is a Completed Call.

---

3 SALES: chalk up a sale for every call that ends with you taking an order.

Suppose you monitor this for a whole week. At the end of the week, the tally sheet will look something like this example:

	Dials	Calls	Sales
Monday	60	30	6
Tuesday	58	26	5
Wednesday	52	24	7
Thursday	66	28	6
Friday	51	21	5
TOTAL	287	129	29

If you monitor a complete quarter, you'll iron out all the bumps caused by holidays, meetings, days off sick and so on, and you'll end up with something like this example:

Dials	Calls	Sales
4,000	2,000	400

Now you just need to know what the total value of those 400 orders amounted to. Suppose each sale is worth £50. That means the total value of those 400 sales is £20,000, which means that you can calculate the value of the dials and completed calls. Clearly they are valuable, because without them you would never make the sales. You can calculate them by dividing the total value of the quarter's sales (£20,000) by the number of dials or completed calls. So for the example above:

- DIALS: £20,000 divided by 4,000 = £5
- C CALLS: £20,000 divided by 2,000 = £10

You can use this formula to calculate the value of your sales calls regularly. It will tell you which members of your sales team are the most productive, which of your lists is most effective, and so on.

Source: John Fenton Training International plc

The time factor

■ *Does it matter whether you use a headset or a handset?*

There's always someone out there trying to sell you the latest piece of equipment, and making all sorts of promises about it. But is it worth investing in equipment that will help to streamline your telemarketing operation, or will it simply eat up all your profits with no clear results to show for it? When it comes to deciding whether to switch your staff over from using handsets to using headsets, the following research finding may help.

- A person using a headset is 43% more productive than a person using a handset.

Source: John Fenton Training International plc

■ How many outbound calls can you get through in an hour?

You can't know whether your telemarketing team is performing well unless you have some idea of how they ought to be performing. Nor can you plan or budget without knowing how many connected calls you can expect a trained sales person to make. Of course, there's a difference between making an after sales call to a consumer and making a sales call to a company director, but the following figures give an average idea of the number of outbound calls you should get through in an hour using a manually operated telephone system.

Consumer	8–15
Business-to-business – switchboard	15
Business-to-business – high level decision makers	2–3

Source: Calcom Associates

Costs

■ How much does telemarketing cost per call?

If you want to get an idea of the total cost of your telemarketing operation, you will have to take into account the cost of staff, equipment, overheads, staff training and so on. Here is a guide to the average cost of each phone call, taking all this into account:

Inbound	£5–10
Outbound	£5–15

Source: Calcom Associates

DIRECT MARKETING

91

MAIL ORDER

Mail order customers

■ *What do consumers see as the benefits of buying through the post?*

Why would you want to buy something without seeing it first? Fortunately for the mail order industry, plenty of people seem to have an answer to this. It's worth knowing the answers because you are at a disadvantage if people are buying from you without seeing the product, and you need to be aware of the compensating benefits so that you can make them as attractive as possible.

Reason	Percentage previous contact with company	Percentage cold
Convenience	41	36
Price	38	28
Not available elsewhere	14	21
Easy to pay/credit	8	7
Can have on approval	7	12
Good quality/good buy	5	2
Saves time	4	–
Good choice/wide range	3	4
Wouldn't have heard of it any other way	3	2
No benefits	3	7

Source: Direct Mail Information Service, 1993

■ *If your prospect knows your company, are they more likely to buy from you?*

The difference is substantial. In fact, people are four times as likely to buy from you through the post if they already know you.

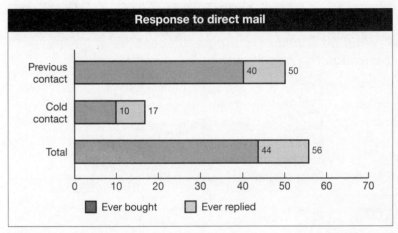

Source: Direct Mail Information Service, 1993

■ *What is stopping your customers buying even more by mail order?*

The Henley Centre research is very clear about one of the key problems that the industry, and individual companies, need to overcome before customers feel completely comfortable buying through the post.

- 40% of the adult population have experience of buying mail order, but 25% of these see control of delivery times as a problem.

Source: The Millennium Post, The Henley Centre, 1995

■ *How much will people spend when they buy by post?*

Obviously it depends on what they are buying, but it is possible to give a general idea of the average spend on different types of products or services. The averages shown in the following chart were reached by asking each respondent how much they spent on each of the last two occasions that they replied to advertising mail and taking an average from these figures. There are two results shown: the figures for all occasions, including those when no money was spent, and the figures only for those occasions when money was spent.

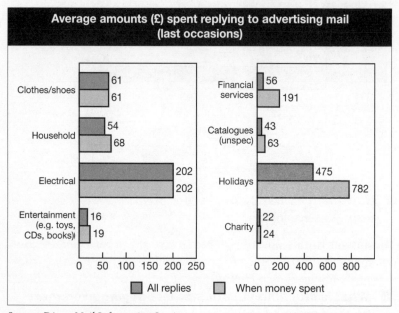

Average amounts (£) spent replying to advertising mail (last occasions)

	All replies	When money spent
Clothes/shoes	61	61
Household	54	68
Electrical	202	202
Entertainment (e.g. toys, CDs, books)	16	19
Financial services	56	191
Catalogues (unspec)	43	63
Holidays	475	782
Charity	22	24

Source: Direct Mail Information Service

■ *Are people satisfied with goods they buy through the mail?*

If people aren't satisfied with their mail order purchases, they may well not buy again (as we'll see in a moment). And it stands to reason that this wariness of buying through the post could extend to other suppliers than the one with whom they had the bad experience. It could put them off buying from you. So it's important for everyone in the industry that consumers should feel comfortable and safe buying through the post. But do they? The DMIS survey indicates that the overall level of satisfaction with goods and services bought through the post is rising.

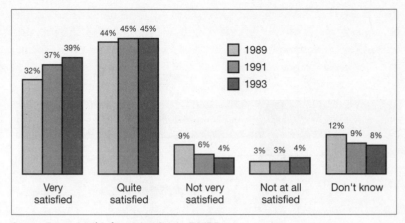

Source: Direct Mail Information Service/BMRB

■ How many unhappy mail order customers will buy from you again?

The answer to this question depends very much on whether your unhappy customers bother to complain. If they don't bother, they will probably not come back for more. However, if they *do* complain, the chances of them buying from you again are increased – even if their complaint isn't resolved satisfactorily. And if you manage to resolve their complaint satisfactorily, they are odds-on to come back to you. So the moral is, it's better to encourage your unhappy customers to complain than to hope that they don't bother you with their problems.

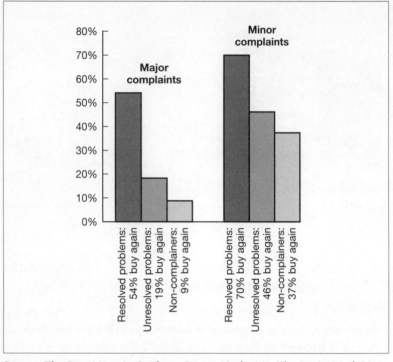

Source: The Practitioner's Guide to Direct Marketing, The Institute of Direct Marketing, 1992

Catalogues

■ *Where does the money go?*

The catalogue is one of the biggest costs of virtually any mail order operation. Since mail order catalogues nowadays have to be packed with colour photographs to be competitive (except in a very few, atypical kinds of business), this is a major expense. As a rule of thumb, you can find out what the paper and printing costs will be, and then double this figure to give you a rough, overall figure for the total production costs. But if you want a slightly clearer idea of where the rest of the money goes, the following list should help. And it's worth noting that it's always wise to have a contingency sum on top.

Item	Percentage of total print cost
Paper	30
Printing	20
Photography	25
Typesetting/artwork	15
Repro-house (colour separation)	10
TOTAL	**100**
Contingencies, add	20

Source: The Practitioner's Guide to Direct Marketing, The Institute of Direct Marketing, 1992

■ How many people who don't place an order straight away do keep your catalogue?

The figure for keeping mail order catalogues is higher than it is for direct mail. In fact, for every person who places an order, around three will hang on to the catalogue for future reference.

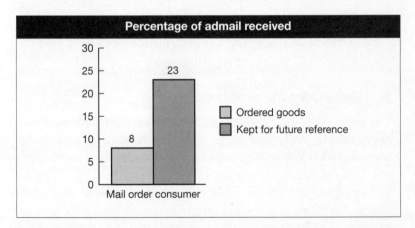

Source: European Society for Opinion and Marketing Research (ESOMAR). This material was first presented at the ESOMAR seminar *Advertising, Sponsorship and Promotions: Understanding and Measuring the Effectiveness of Commercial Communication*, Madrid (Spain), March 1995.

■ *What makes a successful catalogue product?*

Some products are better suited to mail order than others. For example, most of us find it easier to buy frozen peas when we're at the supermarket than to try to order them through the post. So how can you tell which products are likely to sell well by post and which aren't? The following list gives five key factors that have been found to be important; each of your products should have one or more of these attributes:

---

5 key factors for successful catalogue products

1 Difficult to find elsewhere
2 Perceived to be unique
3 Has a 'story' behind it
4 Offers a price advantage
5 Can be bought confidently by mail order.

Source: The Practitioner's Guide to Direct Marketing, The Institute of Direct Marketing, 1992

■ *How many of your catalogue products will succeed?*

Unfortunately, despite the guidelines above, nothing is guaranteed to sell. The failure rate of catalogue products can be high, and you can get a significant number of returns – especially in fashion catalogues, where the number can be as high as 60%. So what proportion of successes should you budget for if you're starting up a mail order business? And if you've been running one for a while, are your failure rates normal? Here's a rule of thumb drawn from research into the success of catalogue products:

- On fashion and higher ticket catalogues:
  - You'll get one third winners
  - You'll get one third break-even products
  - You'll get one third outright losers.
- On lower ticket catalogues:
  - You'll get 20% winners
  - You'll get 60% break-even products
  - You'll get 20% losers.

Source: The Practitioner's Guide to Direct Marketing, The Institute of Direct Marketing, 1992

■ Which are the best selling positions in a catalogue?

Which pages are you using to promote the products that you most want to sell? Some pages catch the reader's attention far more than others, and so tend to be the most successful positions. The best selling positions are:

- The front and back covers
- The inside of the front cover
- The early right hand pages
- The centre spread of the catalogue
- The order forms.

Source: The Practitioner's Guide to Direct Marketing, The Institute of Direct Marketing, 1992

■ How many products should you show on each page?

The more products you put on each page, the more you risk cluttering it to the point where the reader misses individual products. On the other hand, if you only put one item on each page, you'll have very few products to sell (or a very thick catalogue). So where's the happy medium? Fortunately, enough studies have been done that there is an answer to this question.

- Aim for an average of five products per A5 page, but use this on very few pages. Use anything between ten and two. But an average of five will mean that a 32-page catalogue will have better than 150 products.

Source: The Practitioner's Guide to Direct Marketing, The Institute of Direct Marketing, 1992

Business-to-business mail order

■ *How many catalogues do business people receive?*

If you're sending a mail order catalogue to business prospects, it may help to know how many other catalogues they receive. Are you filling a glaring gap in the market, or are you adding to an already flooded one? In fact, you're part of a growing but successful movement: one in ten items of business mail is a catalogue, but they are often used by buyers.

- Only a quarter of recipients say they have never bought through mail order, and a third say they use them for reference but are required to purchase through a central department.

- 66% of respondents have bought from a catalogue in the last 12 months.

- One quarter of all respondents in the DMIS survey had requested a catalogue (rising to 35% for office furniture buyers), and few had asked to be removed from a mailing list.

The following table shows how many catalogues the respondents in the survey had received in the past two months.

1–5	6–10	11–15	16–20	21+
44%	25%	11%	5%	15%
Mean average: 9.1 catalogues				

Source: Direct Mail Information Service

■ Do business people look at the catalogues they receive?

Catalogues are extremely expensive to produce, so you want to know whether they will be looked at and read.

- 82% of targets look at catalogues, even if they only glance at the cover.
- The majority glance through, and 10% look at the catalogue in detail.
- 60% of business targets keep the catalogue until a new one arrives.

Source: Direct Mail Information Service

■ How much do business people spend through catalogues?

How much money do your targets have to spend on your products, and how likely are they to use it to buy through mail order? After all, you want to be sure that if you hook your target, they'll be good for more than a few pence. In fact, the average annual budget available to the catalogue recipients in this survey was £8,641, although 60% of the sample had under £2,500 in their budget. The following table breaks this down into product categories, and indicates what percentage of the total budget is spent through catalogues.

Type of product	Average budget £000's	Percentage spent through catalogues	Percentage spending whole budget	Percentage spending over half budget
Stationery	28	42	15	41
Computer equipment	31	34	12	30
Office furniture	3	34	11	33
Office equipment	8	35	10	32
Retail	17	29	11	26
Warehouse equipment/supplies	1	32	5	29

Source: Direct Mail Information Service

DATABASE MARKETING

Usage

■ Is database marketing efficiently used?

A total of 87% of all respondents agreed that marketing databases will be critical to successful marketing in the future, yet this research shows that only 7% at most are really organised to maximise the benefits of the database marketing approach.

Source: Dataculture, The Henley Centre for Forecasting Ltd, 1997

■ Why is marketing using in-house databases increasing?

If you don't have an in-house database, will you get left behind? Direct Mail Information Services surveyed 148 companies and 50 direct marketing agencies to discover their attitudes towards database marketing. Companies were asked for the main reason for the increased use of in-house databases. Their replies suggested that technological advance is not the only factor.

Reasons for increase	Percentage
More sophisticated technology	28%
More awareness and use in general	20%
More awareness of own database	18%
More awareness of benefits	15%
More funds available	15%

Source: Business Databases – A Study of External Lists and In-House Database Usage, Direct Mail Information Service, 1997

Planning the system

■ *Which types of operations do sales and marketing systems support well?*

If you're thinking of installing a computerised system, you'll want to know which operations you can most effectively use it to support. The Hewson Consulting Group's survey indicated that such systems are considered – by the people who use them – to be much more effective for supporting some functions than others.

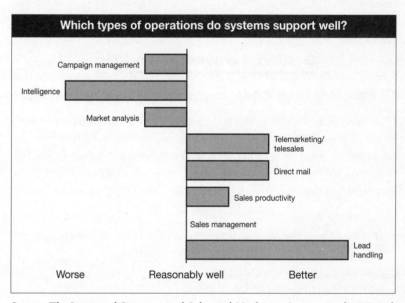

Which types of operations do systems support well?

- Campaign management
- Intelligence
- Market analysis
- Telemarketing/ telesales
- Direct mail
- Sales productivity
- Sales management
- Lead handling

Worse   Reasonably well   Better

Source: The Impact of Computerised Sales and Marketing Systems in the UK (4th Edition), Hewson Consulting Group

■ *Do you need a customised system, or can you manage with off-the-shelf software?*

There's an obvious temptation to use package systems, since they tend to involve less time and expense than customised versions. But should you succumb?

● In fact, there is a growing tendency to use package systems which is not confined to small companies. 80% of companies in the survey were using an off-the-shelf system.

Source: The Impact of Computerised Sales and Marketing Systems in the UK (4th Edition), Hewson Consulting Group

Getting the system working

■ *How long does it take to get your system operational?*

This factor can be crucial to the success of your business when you install a new system. If you're still in the process of getting yours operational, are you starting to wonder if everyone takes as long as you? For one thing, there is a correlation between the number of system users and the time it takes to get the thing up and running smoothly – the more users, the longer it takes.

● In this survey, the longest time any system took to get operational was five years, but the average was 18 months.

Source: The Impact of Computerised Sales and Marketing Systems in the UK (4th Edition), Hewson Consulting Group

■ *What are the biggest barriers to using a sales and marketing system effectively?*

An effective system can be the key to success, but an ineffective one is a drain on both resources and morale. The biggest single barrier to effectiveness quoted by survey respondents was lack of motivation among the key players. Several other factors also played an important role.

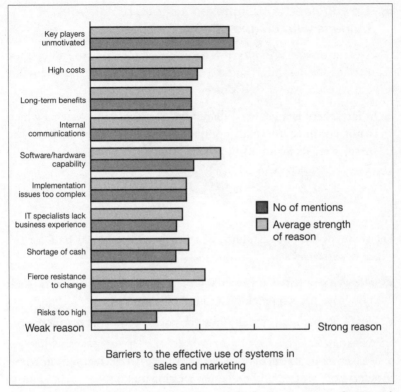

Key players unmotivated

High costs

Long-term benefits

Internal communications

Software/hardware capability

Implementation issues too complex

IT specialists lack business experience

Shortage of cash

Fierce resistance to change

Risks too high

Weak reason _____ Strong reason

■ No of mentions
□ Average strength of reason

Barriers to the effective use of systems in sales and marketing

Source: The Impact of Computerised Sales and Marketing Systems in the UK (4th Edition), Hewson Consulting Group

The costs

■ Which department pays the capital costs of the system?

If you're considering setting up a computerised sales and marketing system, you may be wondering whose budget the capital costs will come out of. The main contenders are the marketing department, sales department, IT/IS, and special or project budgets. The allocation of capital costs by companies in this survey is shown in the following diagram.

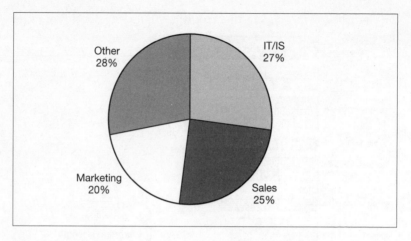

The survey went on to establish which type of system was paid for by which department:

- **Sales departments** tended to pay the capital costs of systems used to improve decision making and use of resources.
- **The IT/IS** budget generally met the costs of systems for increased sales.
- **Marketing departments** usually paid for systems focused on competitive advantage, and on better decision making.
- The question of who pays is often determined by the function of the system's sponsor, or driving force. When the system was driven by a board level sponsor, it tended to be paid for out of a special or project budget.

Source: The Impact of Computerised Sales and Marketing Systems in the UK (4th Edition), Hewson Consulting Group

■ *What are the major costs involved in setting up a sales and marketing system?*

The direct costs – the hardware and software – only amount to about 45% of the total cost of the system. Most of the companies in the survey had not taken the hidden costs into account at all – the time spent training, the loss of selling time while staff are adjusting to the system, and so on. Consequently, the research company was obliged to estimate these indirect costs on the basis of what they could glean from the respondents. They did this on a very conservative basis, so the chart below has underestimated, if anything, the contribution of these costs.

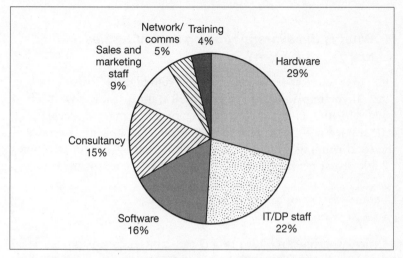

Source: *The Impact of Computerised Sales and Marketing Systems in the UK (4th Edition)*, Hewson Consulting Group

■ *What will a computerised system cost?*

So much for percentages and contributions; what's the bottom line in hard cash terms? If you don't know that, it's impossible to assess whether it will be cost effective to install one. The survey measured the capital costs in terms of the cost per system user, and came up with an average of £4,800. This breaks down as follows:

Breakdown of costs	£ per user
Hardware	1,400
Software	800
Networks and communications	250
External consultancy	720
Training – trainer's costs	180
IT/DP staff	1,050
User time in training etc.	400

Source: *The Impact of Computerised Sales and Marketing Systems in the UK (4th Edition)*, Hewson Consulting Group

It's worth noting that many companies do not, in fact, have to pay any hardware costs since they can install a new system to run on existing hardware.

■ What is the average running cost of a sales and marketing system?

Of course, once your system is up and running, the costs don't stop there. If you're planning a system, you'll want to know how much to budget for the on-going costs of keeping it maintained, keeping the staff trained and so on. Hewson Consulting Group's study estimated the total running costs of a sales and marketing system at around £2,300 a year per user, which breaks down in the following way:

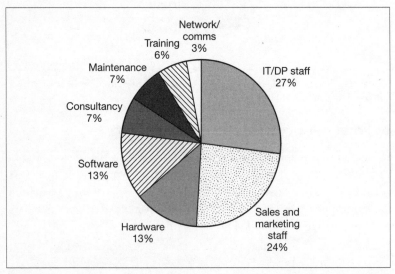

Source: *The Impact of Computerised Sales and Marketing Systems in the UK (4th Edition),* Hewson Consulting Group

■ What is the typical payback time?

This is the $64,000 question; the one that asks 'is it worth it?' If the system is generating enough revenue that couldn't have been achieved without it, you'll be much more willing to forgive it its capital costs. Hewson Consulting Group's study found nine companies which were able to put figures on the benefits of their systems. Five of these nine systems had paid back within a year, as you can see from the following table which details all nine systems.

Company	Total users	Costs	Benefits	Payback
Manufacturer Turnover £5–20m	2	Capital £5.5k Annual £2k	Better use of resources £5k pa	1¾ years
Information technology Turnover £5–20m	20	Capital £33k Annual £7.5k	Better decision making £10k pa Cost reduction £10k pa Competitive advantage £10k pa	1¾ years
Information technology Turnover under £5m	6	Capital £11.3k Annual £11.3k	Increased sales & market share £250k pa Customer retention £300k pa	¼ year
Business services Turnover over £250m	21	Capital £163k Annual £72.5k	Cost reduction £50k pa Better use of existing resources £70k pa	3½ years
Information technology Turnover £21–50m	14	Capital £55k Annual £72k	Increased sales £756k pa Customer retention £210k pa plus £840k one-off	¼ year
Capital goods Turnover £5–20m	16	Capital £96k Annual £35k	Increased sales £500k pa	¼ year
Capital goods Turnover £21–50m	56	Capital £413k Annual £60k	Cost reduction & better use of existing resources £48k pa Increased sales & market share £140k pa Competitive advantage £12k pa	3 years
Pharm. & healthcare Turnover £21–50m	32	Capital £154k Annual £60k	Increased sales & market share £800k pa Cost reduction £20k pa	¼ year
Distribution	110	Capital £450k Annual £42k	Ability to cross sell £750k pa Cost reduction £55k pa	¾ year

Source: The Impact of Computerised Sales and Marketing Systems in the UK (4th Edition), Hewson Consulting Group

DIRECT MARKETING

109

Hewson Consulting Group investigated the five companies with the fastest payback, to see whether there were any common themes. There was a wide variation in the number of users, type of software, cost per user, length of set-up time and seniority of the sponsor. The only unifying factors they could find were:

- All the systems were designed and implemented by highly computer-literate project managers, whether in sales, marketing or IT.

- Their primary objectives were all focused on revenue growth or maintenance; none of them was driven by cost reduction.

Source: The Impact of Computerised Sales and Marketing Systems in the UK (4th Edition), Hewson Consulting Group

Mailing lists

■ *Which types of mailing lists get the best response?*

There are plenty of places you can get a mailing list. Where it comes from will affect the response rate you get to your mailing. Essentially there are three sources:

- Your customers
- Your prospects (names you have collected as a result of enquiries, visits to your exhibition stand or whatever)
- Rented lists.

So how much will your response rates vary according to which list you use?

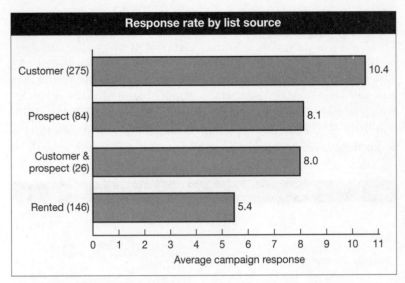

Response rate by list source

Customer (275) — 10.4
Prospect (84) — 8.1
Customer & prospect (26) — 8.0
Rented (146) — 5.4

0 1 2 3 4 5 6 7 8 9 10 11
Average campaign response

Source: Direct Mail Information Service

■ How can you assess the value of a list you're considering using?

The cost of renting or buying lists can add up, especially if you want a lot of names. Even if you use your own list, the production and mailing costs are high, so you want to be sure that you're using the best list you can. But how do you evaluate a list? Here are a few rules of thumb.

● Your own customers are 3 to 8 times more likely to buy from you than anyone else's customers whose names you buy.

● The world is divided into people who buy mail order and people who just don't. So if a list is made up of people who have bought mail order in the past, they are much more likely to do so again.

If you compare a successful list with a new one you're thinking of using, you can predict whether it will work:

● If the duplication factor between the two lists is 25%, your mailing has about an 86% chance of succeeding.

● If the duplication factor is under 10%, the likelihood of a successful mailing is about 3%.

Source: The Drayton Bird Partnership

DIRECT MARKETING

■ *What do people think you're going to do with their name and address?*

Many people are very knowledgeable about what you are likely to do with their details. However, a significant minority do not realise that you will keep a record of them, and possibly mail them again, or even pass their details on to other companies. It is worth being aware that these people are not expecting to find that personal information about them is being shared.

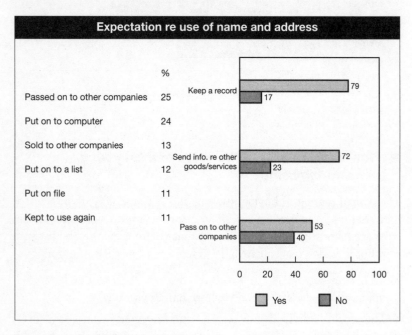

Expectation re use of name and address

	%
Passed on to other companies	25
Put on to computer	24
Sold to other companies	13
Put on to a list	12
Put on file	11
Kept to use again	11

Source: Direct Mail Information Service

■ Do you tell people what you are going to do with their personal details?

A growing number of companies is stating clearly what will happen to any names and addresses held on file. The percentage of mailshots that give a notification of future marketing is:

Explain future use of list	30.9%
Give opt-out from details being re-used/passed on	27.3%
Mention Data Protection Act	10.1%
Mention Mailing Preference Service	1%

Source: Direct Mail Services Standards Board, 1993/4

■ Do people know about consumer protection schemes and legislation?

A fairly high number of consumers are well aware that legislation exists to protect them. Many of them know of the Data Protection Act and the organisations that exist to protect their privacy. If they know that these rules exist, you are more likely to increase their trust than to confuse or worry them by giving them more information.

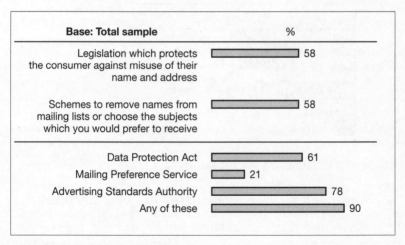

Base: Total sample	%
Legislation which protects the consumer against misuse of their name and address	58
Schemes to remove names from mailing lists or choose the subjects which you would prefer to receive	58
Data Protection Act	61
Mailing Preference Service	21
Advertising Standards Authority	78
Any of these	90

Source: Direct Mail Information Service

DIRECT MARKETING

Business-to-business mailing lists

■ Which external lists are most widely used?

Where do you go to rent a mailing list? The most widely rented external lists are directories, used by 57% of business-to-business marketing departments. Most businesses use a variety of external sources – directories, subscription lists, membership lists, compiled response lists and exhibition lists.

Source: Business Databases – A Study of External Lists and In-House Database Usage, Direct Mail Information Service, 1997

■ How many names do you mail in the average mailing?

Effective business direct mail is generally a low-volume activity. The target market is usually highly defined, and even prospecting is a very targeted activity. Across the sectors surveyed, the average volume of names mailed in 1995 was 600,000 – but the picture varies dramatically by sector:

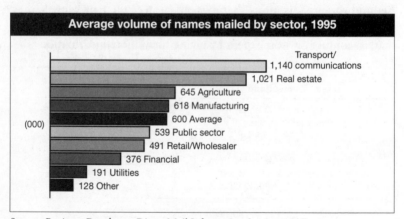

Average volume of names mailed by sector, 1995

- Transport/communications 1,140
- 1,021 Real estate
- 645 Agriculture
- 618 Manufacturing
- 600 Average
- 539 Public sector
- 491 Retail/Wholesaler
- 376 Financial
- 191 Utilities
- 128 Other

(000)

Source: Business Databases, Direct Mail Information Service, 1997

■ How much do other businesses use external lists?

If you're considering using external lists, it may help you to know how many other businesses do, and what balance of internal and external list they use. External rental list volume is relatively evenly spread; half of business marketers rented fewer than 100,000 names in 1995.

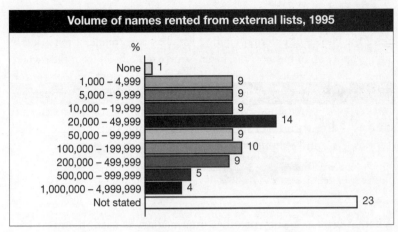

Volume of names rented from external lists, 1995

%	
None	1
1,000 – 4,999	9
5,000 – 9,999	9
10,000 – 19,999	9
20,000 – 49,999	14
50,000 – 99,999	9
100,000 – 199,999	10
200,000 – 499,999	9
500,000 – 999,999	5
1,000,000 – 4,999,999	4
Not stated	23

Source: Business Databases, Direct Mail Information Service, 1997

■ What balance of external and internal data does your company use?

Combining external lists with internal data is the most common way for business marketers to put together their mailing lists. As many as 65% use this approach. The average split between each source is 44% external to 56% internal. Over a quarter of marketers used between five and eight rented names in every ten mailed. The average rate of duplication between external and internal databases is 16%.

Source: Business Databases, Direct Mail Information Service, 1997

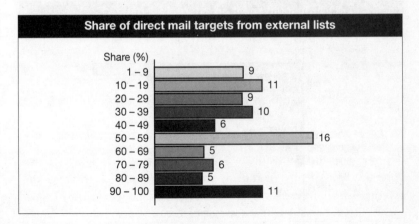

Share of direct mail targets from external lists

Share (%)	
1 – 9	9
10 – 19	11
20 – 29	9
30 – 39	10
40 – 49	6
50 – 59	16
60 – 69	5
70 – 79	6
80 – 89	5
90 – 100	11

Source: Business Databases, Direct Mail Information Service, 1997

DIRECT MARKETING

■ *Who do companies rent their external lists through?*

Once the choice of external mailing lists has been made, a remarkably high proportion of business marketers source data direct from the owner:

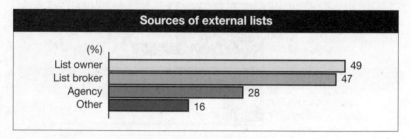

Where a broker, agency or other intermediary is used, the main reasons cited are:

- Expertise   49%
- Convenience   37%.

Source: Business Databases, Direct Mail Information Service, 1997

■ *What is the average expenditure on external lists?*

If you use external lists, it's worth knowing how much other companies spend on external data. The average expenditure in 1995 on external lists was £65,000, although half of the companies surveyed spent less than £10,000.

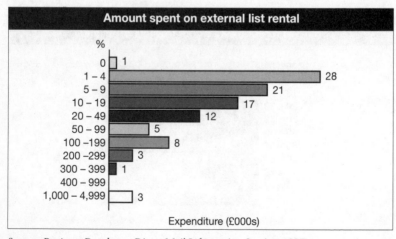

Source: Business Databases, Direct Mail Information Service, 1997

■ *How do you select your external mailing lists?*

You may think that the frequency of updating is crucial to your choice of mailing lists. Do other companies think the same? List users see data quality issues as the most important factors influencing their choice. Updating, validating and postcoding were the most important. Cost was rated only fifth.

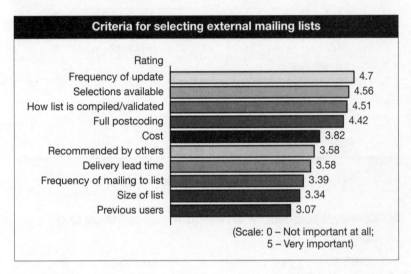

Criteria for selecting external mailing lists

	Rating
Frequency of update	4.7
Selections available	4.56
How list is compiled/validated	4.51
Full postcoding	4.42
Cost	3.82
Recommended by others	3.58
Delivery lead time	3.58
Frequency of mailing to list	3.39
Size of list	3.34
Previous users	3.07

(Scale: 0 – Not important at all;
5 – Very important)

Source: Business Databases, Direct Mail Information Service, 1997

■ *How accurate are business mailing lists?*

Do you merge and purge regularly (if you'll pardon the expression)? Inaccuracies can mean that your mailshot never reaches your prospect or – if it does – it's likely to irritate them. Worryingly, though, errors in addressing direct mail items seem to be on the increase.

DIRECT MARKETING

Error	Percentage of items received	
	1991	**1994**
Name wrong/spelt wrongly	4	9
Personal title wrong	5	4
Job title wrong	6	6
Department missed out/wrong	5	5
Company name wrong/spelt wrongly	4	7
Wrong address	5	5
Name/title/address out of date	8	17
% Errors	37	53

Source: Direct Mail Information Service

USING AN AGENCY

■ On what basis do you pay your direct marketing agency?

You don't have to pay a straight fee, and many companies don't. So what does everyone else do? One survey of large companies from a cross-section of industries showed that although the most common method of payment is by a straight fee, other methods are used as well. (A few companies use more than one method of payment, which is why the percentages add up to more than 100.)

Payment for results	3%
Commission/percentage	4%
Straight fees	46%
Payment for ideas	4%
Other methods	4%
Not stated	41%

Source: Richmond Events Limited

■ *How often should you review your relationship with your direct marketing agency?*

A regular review session with your agency will bring any problems to light and make sure that your relationship is still as fruitful as it should be. But what is 'regular'? Should you be planning a review every five years, or hauling them into your office every other week? The table below will give you a clue as to what is the norm.

Annually	14%
Every six months	6%
Every quarter	3%
Continually – project by project	15%
No fixed period of time	21%
Not applicable	19%
Not stated	22%

Source: Richmond Events Limited

ADVERTISING

DIFFERENT MEDIA

■ Do the appropriate advertising media vary by product sector?

What media do your competitors favour for advertising? Consumers are involved in a wide range of purchases. Do they look to different media for information about different products? This chart shows which media are used most in each sector

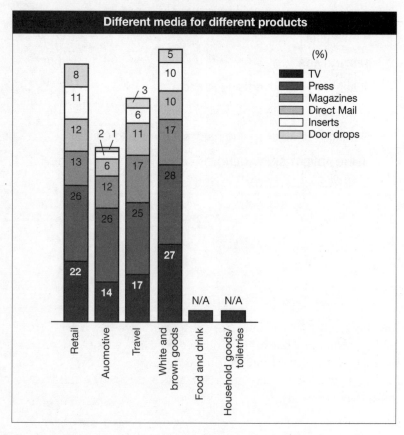

Different media for different products

Source: *DMIS Intelligence Sector Reports*, Direct Mail Information Service, 1997

■ *What advertising influences your customers when they are shopping?*

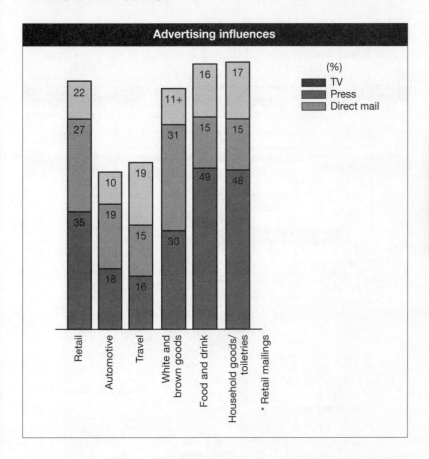

Advertising influences

The impact of each medium also varies with product price. Direct mail, for example, has more influence on consumers if the price is lower. It is the second most influential major advertising medium for lower ticket items like groceries, and is the most influential in travel purchases.

Source: *DMIS Intelligence Sector Reports*, Direct Mail Information Service, 1997

ADVERTISING

123

■ How do people's attitudes to different media vary?

Television advertising is still considered to be the most persuasive medium, with 60% of consumers assigning it this quality. Direct mail is still seen as intrusive by nearly 2 in 5 consumers; it could be argued that this is the very quality which makes it attractive to marketers.

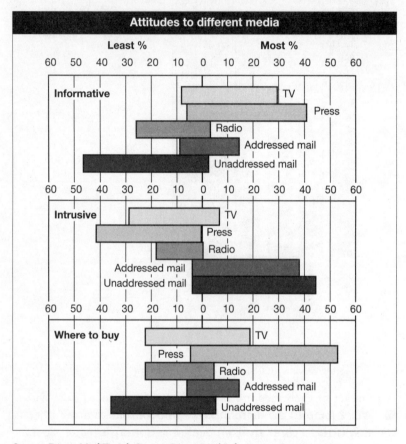

Source: *Direct Mail Trends Survey*, Direct Mail Information Service, 1997

■ Which advertising medium should you use?

Different media have different strengths and weaknesses, which will determine which ones you use for any particular campaign. The applications vary, as do the degree of targeting, the costs, the responses and so on. Here's a very broad assessment of media strengths and weaknesses.

Medium	Applications	Targeting	Testing	Cost (per contact)	Speed – Mount	Speed – Response (cumulative)	Response – Percent	Response – Volume
Direct mail	All. Weakest on recruitment of cold prospects, especially where no suitable list available.	V. good	V. good	V. high	Slow	Medium	High	Medium
Inserts	Lead generation; direct sales, especially continuity offers and non cash-with-order sales.	Good	V. good	Low to medium	Medium	Fast	Medium to low	High
Press	Lead generation; direct sales; general awareness; support for other direct activities; store traffic.	Medium	Medium	V. low	Fast	Fast	Low	High
Posters	Awareness; store traffic boost.	Poor	Nil	V. low	Slow	Slow	Nil	Nil
TV – general	Awareness; store traffic boost.	Medium to poor	Poor	High	Fast	Fast	Low	Low
TV – direct response	Lead generation (high ticket items); direct sales (low ticket); support for other direct activities.	Medium	Poor	Low	Fast	Fast	Low	Medium
Radio	Awareness; store and event traffic boost; lead generation (high ticket business-to-business).	Medium to poor	Poor	High	V. fast	Medium	V. low	Low

Source: *The Practitioner's Guide to Direct Marketing*, The Institute of Direct Marketing, 1992

■ *What type of advertising are people most likely to respond to directly?*

Many ads, of course, have a slow build-up effect. It takes the viewer or listener a while to develop a sufficient awareness of the product or service to go out and buy it. Sometimes this awareness is generated by a number of different ads in various media. However, there are times when the decision to go out and buy is directly stimulated by a specific ad. This chart is taken from a survey in which people were asked about enquiries or purchases they had made as a direct result of hearing about a product or service.

125

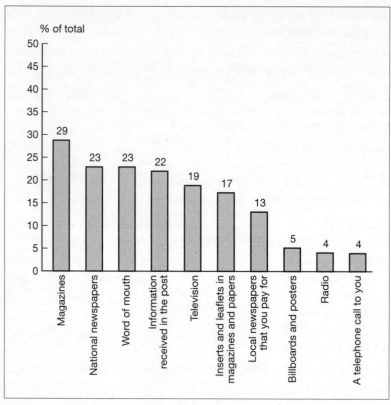

% of total

Source: *The Millennium Post*, The Henley Centre, 1995

TV advertising

■ *How often should you run a TV ad?*

TV advertising is bought in 'television ratings', or TVRs. The number of TVRs you buy indicates what percentage of the potential audience will see your ad once. So 30 Adult TVRs will mean that 30% of the adults in the region to which you are broadcasting will see the ad once. Different advertising spots are, of course, worth a different number of TVRs.

If you keep showing the ad, it will be seen more times. This happens in two ways: more people see the ad, or the same people see it more often. For this reason, if you buy over 100 TVRs it doesn't mean that over 100% of people will see the ad. It means that some people will have more than one 'opportunity to see', or OTS as the jargon has it. For example, if you buy 400 TVRs, you should find that 80% of people have 5 opportunities to see it (80 × 5 = 400). So how many TVRs should you buy to make your television ads worth while?

- Aim for at least 70% coverage (that's around 250–300 TVRs).

- Aim for a minimum OTS of at least 4.

Source: The Drayton Bird Partnership

■ Does it make any difference how long the break is during which your ad is shown?

As a rule, the viewer doesn't know how long the commercial break they are watching is going to go on for, so why should it make any difference to whether your ad makes an impact? There are two factors at work here: whether the audience keeps watching (rather than getting bored and wandering off), and whether they continue to take in what they're seeing. The evidence of the research below indicates that while a few of them wander off, the greatest factor is that the more ads they see, the lower their recall of each one. The chart gives an index value of 100 to the recall rating of the first spot in the break.

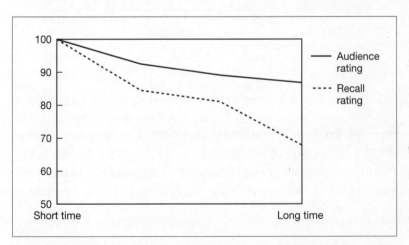

Source: European Society for Opinion and Marketing Research (ESOMAR). This material was first presented at the ESOMAR seminar *Advertising, Sponsorship and Promotions: Understanding and Measuring the Effectiveness of Commercial Communication*, Madrid (Spain), March 1995.

127

■ *What time of day will give you the best response to your ad?*

Direct response television advertising, in which you ask the viewer to contact you to make an enquiry or to place an order, is a very fast growing market. There are numerous techniques you can use to get the best response possible. For a start, people are more likely to respond to a daytime ad. The following table, indexed on the average for all parts of the day, shows how much more responsive daytime audiences are.

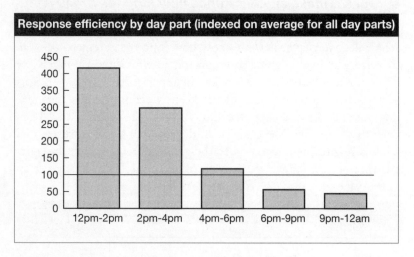

Response efficiency by day part (indexed on average for all day parts)

Source: *Ch4/BT Joint Research 1994* – Based on 1993 commercials

This is good news, because daytime ads have a lower TVR and are therefore cheaper. But it's not as simple as that, because some days of the week get better responses than others. The following table is indexed on the average for the week.

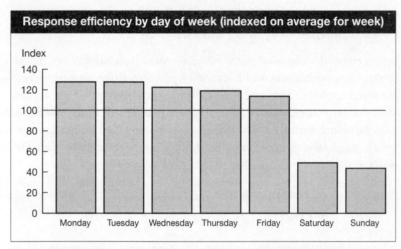

Source: *Ch4/BT Joint Research 1994* – Based on 1993 commercials

■ *How long should your ad run?*

Very short ads can be effective, but in general the longer the ad, the better the response you will get from it.

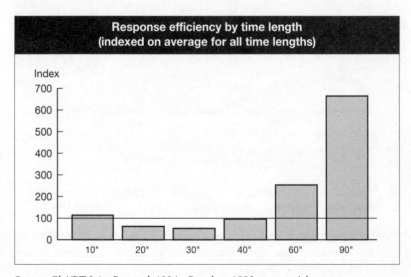

Source: *Ch4/BT Joint Research 1994* – Based on 1993 commercials

ADVERTISING

■ Should you advertise during a break in the middle of a programme, or at the end of it?

It is generally reckoned that viewers will watch the breaks in the middle of programmes to be sure they don't miss the second half. If they want to put the kettle on, they'll wait until the end break. However, if you're asking viewers for a direct response to your ad, it seems to work the other way round – which is good news, since centre breaks tend to be cheaper. The reason appears to be that people who don't want to miss the second half of their programme don't want to start hunting for pens and paper during the centre break – let alone making phone calls to you. By the end of the programme – if you advertised in the middle of it – they will have forgotten your number.

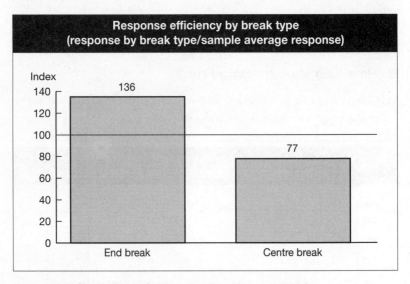

Source: *Ch4/BT Joint Research 1994* – Based on 1993 commercials

■ How can you encourage people to contact you when they see your ad?

You need to make it easy for people. Give them a phone number to call – preferably a free one. But how can you make the most of the phone number when you design the ad? There are two key factors – whether you say the phone number as well as showing it on the screen, and how long the number is on the screen.

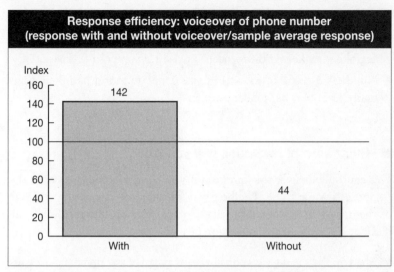

Source: *Ch4/BT Joint Research 1994* – Based on 1993 commercials

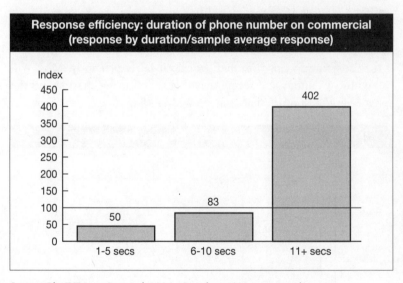

Source: *Ch4/BT Joint Research 1994* – Based on 1993 commercials

ADVERTISING

■ *How big should the phone number be?*

You might well think that as long as the number is large enough to be legible, it makes no difference. But research shows otherwise.

- Numbers 6–10% of the screen size generate more than 3 times as many responses as smaller numbers.

Source: *Ch4/BT Joint Research 1995*

■ *What kind of response will you get?*

You can only answer this question if you have some idea of what the response is going to be. The best way to calculate it is as a percentage of the audience that actually sees the ad. Here are the results of one piece of research among television advertisers.

- The top 10 average response rate was 0.18% – that's 1,800 calls per 1,000,000 audience.

Source: *Ch4/BT Joint Research 1995*

■ *How quickly will people respond?*

If they're going to call you, they will do it fairly promptly. Most will call within 15 minutes of seeing the ad. The following chart shows the spread of the responses that come in within 45 minutes of the spot.

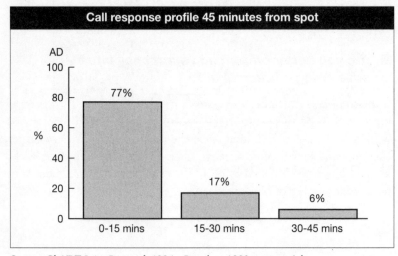

Source: *Ch4/BT Joint Research 1994* – Based on 1993 commercials

■ Can you handle the response?

It's frightening how many companies just aren't prepared for the response to a TV ad. One company answered 1,200 calls during a campaign and lost 54,000. It had hooked its number up to an answering machine. The latest research showed that:

- 63% of calls in response to ads were answered.

- 37% were lost, chiefly due to lack of call handling resources.

- The researchers removed 8 'rogue' campaigns from the figures; this still left a call failure rate of 23%.

Source: Ch4/BT Joint Research 1995

■ What does direct response TV advertising say about you?

There was a time when this type of advertising was seen to be down-market. However, attitudes seem to be changing. The impression it gives of your company these days is:

- You are approachable, and want to be accessible to your customers.

- You are organised and financially sound, with quality products.

Source: Ch4/BT Joint Research 1995

■ Are you better off putting your money into TV advertising or direct mail?

It depends very much on what you're trying to achieve. TV advertising seems to be the most effective way to raise brand awareness, while direct mail is reckoned to be the most effective way to target customers. A survey of advertisers came up with the following views of the comparative benefits of TV advertising and direct mail, in terms of a number of objectives.

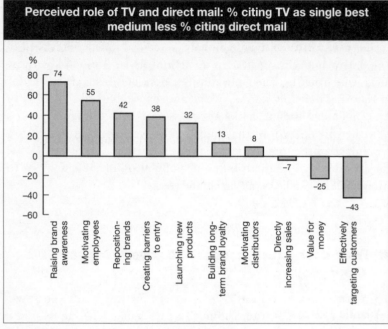

Perceived role of TV and direct mail: % citing TV as single best medium less % citing direct mail

Source: *The Henley Centre Survey of Advertisers 1993*

Radio advertising

■ *How many people listen to commercial radio?*

If you're thinking of advertising on radio, the first thing you'll need to know is who is going to hear your advertisement. The answers are encouraging – most people listen to commercial radio.

- In any one week, 61% of the population (aged 15 and over) listen to commercial radio.
- The average length of time each of these people spends listening is almost 15 hours a week.
- 27% of the population listen to national commercial radio during the course of a week.
- 49% of the population listen to local commercial radio during the course of a week.

Source: Radio Joint Audience Research Limited, Quarter 3, 1995

■ *Which national radio stations attract the most listeners?*

If you want to advertise on national commercial radio, you'll need to know how many people listen to each radio station, and for how long. This won't be your only consideration, but it is a crucial factor in choosing the right station. We've already established that 27% of the population listen to national commercial radio each week; here's a further breakdown of that figure. (The weekly reach shown is a percentage of the total population, not a fraction of those 27%. So, for example, 7% of the total adult population of the UK listen to Atlantic 252 at some point during the week.)

Radio station	Weekly reach		Average hours		Total hours
	'000	%	per head	per listener	'000
Atlantic 252	3,465	7	0.4	5.7	19,648
Classic FM	4,734	10	0.6	5.7	26,819
Talk Radio UK	2,162	5	0.3	6.7	14,501
Virgin Radio (AM only)	2,890	6	0.5	2.4	21,394

Source: Radio Joint Audience Research Limited, Quarter 3, 1995

■ *What type of people listen to commercial radio?*

Numbers alone aren't that much use, of course. You also need to know whether the radio listener profile matches your target audience.

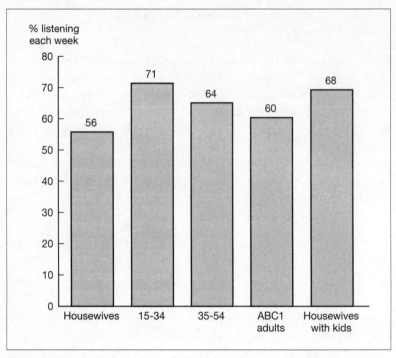

% listening
each week

Source: Radio Joint Audience Research Limited / Radio Advertising Bureau

■ *Is radio any use for advertising to business people?*

- Almost 70% of business people listen to commercial radio during the course of a week.

Source: Radio Advertising Bureau

To give you some idea of how this compares with other advertising media, the following table shows the weekly reach of some of the most common ways to advertise to business people.

Advertising media	Weekly reach	
	'000s	%
Any commercial radio	810	69
Classic FM	294	25
Daily Telegraph	394	33
Financial Times	342	29
Capital FM	198	17
London Underground	229	19
The Times	373	32

*BASE: All business people 1,178,000

Source: *The British Business Survey 1995*, Research Services Limited

■ *Do people switch off when the ads come on?*

Television viewers are notorious for zapping out the ads. But radio listeners rarely bother. So if they're tuned in, they're far more likely to hear what you have to say.

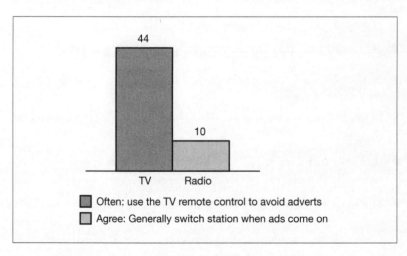

Source: *Media Futures*, The Henley Centre, 1993

ADVERTISING

■ What does advertising on radio say about you?

People have different images of different media – the television, for example, is seen as being very glamorous. These images rub off on the advertisers who choose to use each particular medium. So what image do you automatically acquire by choosing to advertise on radio?

- People see radio as being very close to them, and the 'same size' as themselves. It's an intimate medium, and it gives your relationship with the listener a more personal feel.

- People are more likely to believe what they hear on the radio than on television, and this includes the ads.

- National radio stations are aimed at a particular kind of listener, and this image attaches itself to you when you advertise on that station. For example, Classic FM is seen to be aimed at the more educated, sophisticated person.

- Local radio is regarded as being on the same level as the listeners. It doesn't talk down to them, or try to be bigger and better than they are. This gives it a friendly, 'people like me' feel.

Source: Radio Advertising Bureau

■ Do people take in radio ads?

You would probably expect that people would take little notice of radio ads. After all, they're usually doing something else when the radio is on. But in fact:

- People's ability to remember ads when prompted is 80% of what it is for television.

- Different techniques, such as dialogue, mood, drama and so on, can make as much as 300% difference to how memorable the ad is.

- The most effective radio ads are the ones that involve the listeners and get an emotional response from them. People like ads to be enjoyable or interesting, and this gives them a positive attitude towards you and your product or service.

Source: Radio Advertising Bureau

■ *How many times will each listener hear your ad?*

If you run an average weight campaign, your ad will be heard by each consumer listening about four times a week, on average. This compares with about one 'impact' for television or press ads.

A television ad will, on average, reach each buyer only once per week (see the following table):

<table>
<tr><td colspan="7" align="center">APRIL</td></tr>
<tr><td>Mon</td><td>Tues</td><td>Wed</td><td>Thurs</td><td>Fri</td><td>Sat</td><td>Sun</td></tr>
<tr><td></td><td></td><td></td><td></td><td>1 📺</td><td>2</td><td>3</td></tr>
<tr><td>4</td><td>5</td><td>6</td><td>7</td><td>8</td><td>9</td><td>10</td></tr>
<tr><td>11</td><td>12 📺</td><td>13</td><td>14</td><td>15</td><td>16</td><td>17</td></tr>
<tr><td>18</td><td>19</td><td>20 📺</td><td>21</td><td>22</td><td>23</td><td>24</td></tr>
<tr><td>25</td><td>26</td><td>27</td><td>28</td><td>29 📺</td><td>30</td><td></td></tr>
</table>

Television ad exposure ('average' campaign weight)

Source: Radio Advertising Bureau

ADVERTISING

An average radio campaign delivers about four 'impacts' each week:

APRIL						
Mon	Tues	Wed	Thurs	Fri	Sat	Sun
				1 📻	2 📻	3
4 📻	5	6 📻	7 📻	8	9	10 📻
11 📻	12	13 📻	14	15	16 📻	17
18 📻	19 📻	20	21 📻	22	23 📻	24
25 📻	26 📻	27	28 📻	29	30 📻	

📻 Radio ad exposure ('average' campaign weight)

Source: Radio Advertising Bureau

Press advertising

■ *How often should you run a press ad?*

You don't want to waste your money, but you want the best coverage possible. There are no clear-cut rules, but as a guideline for getting the best from your press advertising:

- The smaller the ad, the more often you may repeat.
- The more interesting a product, the more often it can run.
- The larger the circulation, the more often you may repeat.

Source: The Drayton Bird Partnership

■ For direct response advertising, what effect does frequency have on response rate?

At least with a direct response ad you can tell whether your ads are still being read by prospects. But it's worth being prepared for the drop-off in response before you start the campaign. It will have all sorts of budgeting and planning implications.

Direct response advertising follows the law of diminishing returns. Assuming that all other factors are equal (such as seasonality, for example), awareness of the company or the offer will increase as the responses to individual ads fall.

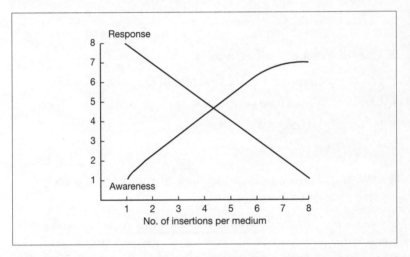

Source: *The Practitioner's Guide to Direct Marketing*, The Institute of Direct Marketing, 1992

■ When is the best time to place an ad?

Your particular product or service may well dictate certain advertising times. You won't do so well, for example, advertising bathing costumes in November as you will in late spring. But, if your product isn't seasonal, there are certain rules of thumb worth knowing about:

- Winter is generally better than summer.

- January and September are usually the best months.

- Test your ads on particular days of the week – it can make a difference.

Source: The Drayton Bird Partnership

■ *Which are the most effective advertising positions?*

The spaces that do best will cost you more, of course, but you get what you pay for. The best positions in magazines and newspapers are:

- Front cover, followed by back cover
- Front of publication is better than back
- Right hand pages are generally better than left
- Pages facing editorial generally do better than others (but test it)
- Positions next to letters, TV listings or horoscopes do well
- Special supplements which are relevant pay.

Source: The Drayton Bird Partnership

■ *...and the least effective?*

- Gutter positions (near the central fold of the publication)
- Late in the publication surrounded by other ads
- Surrounded by editorial.

Source: The Drayton Bird Partnership

■ *What difference does the size of the ad make to the response?*

If you want a direct response to your ads, the frequency with which you run the ad will affect the response, as we have already seen. The response drops every time you repeat the ad. The standard way to deal with this is to stop advertising in that particular publication for a while, and then start again once the offer appears fresh again (you'll only know how long that is by testing; it varies widely according to the offer).

So you want to be able to reduce the frequency of your ads in a way that has the smallest possible effect on the total volume of the response. And one of the best ways to do that is to take larger spaces. The following chart shows the effect on response of increasing the space size. The number of replies are given as a percentage of the number of replies that a full page ad would generate. So, for instance, a quarter page ad should generate 25% of the replies that a full page ad would.

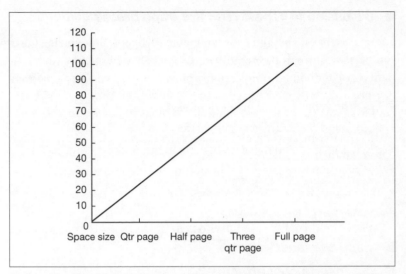

Source: *The Practitioner's Guide to Direct Marketing*, The Institute of Direct Marketing, 1992

■ On which page of a local paper is your advertisement most likely to be seen?

To answer this, you need to know which pages are most likely to be read. Then you can place your ad on, or opposite, those pages (unless, of course, it is specifically appropriate to some other page). So which types of editorial get most read?

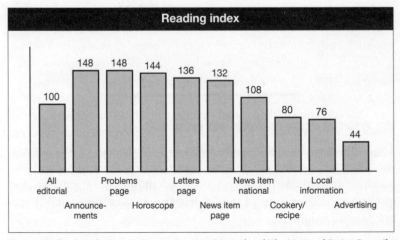

Source: Welbeck Golin/Harris Communications Limited and The National Dairy Council

143

■ *Do business people read the trade press?*

Clearly, one of the best targeted ways to reach your business prospects is through their trade press. You can get hold of circulation figures for individual publications. However, you can't assume that just because someone subscribes to a publication, they automatically read it. It's worth bearing in mind the findings of one survey:

- 38% of business people in the survey said they did not have time to read their specific trade press.

Source: Direct Mail Information Service

Inserts

■ *Are inserts cost effective?*

Is it really worth the cost of printing leaflets to insert into magazines and newspapers? It's far cheaper just to place an ad, isn't it? Well yes, it is cheaper. But the evidence is that the cost benefits of inserts outweigh the cost disadvantages.

- Inserts usually work out at around 4 or 5 times more expensive than advertising space.
- Inserts pull up to 5 or 6 times more response than a full-page advertisement.

Source: *The Practitioner's Guide to Direct Marketing*, The Institute of Direct Marketing, 1992

Door-to-door advertising

■ *What is door-to-door advertising?*

This is the term used for putting leaflets through doors using specialist distribution companies, the Royal Mail, local newspaper delivery people and so on. It is similar to direct mail, except that the leaflets are not addressed to a named individual (which can make it less effective, especially for business-to-business advertising). In terms of its effectiveness, the main points to bear in mind are:

- It usually works out at around half the cost of direct mail.

- You can target addresses with particular postcodes. This means you can break down local areas into small groups of households with likely common characteristics.

- Door-to-door advertising works well in support of other marketing techniques, such as a sales force in the area, or a television advertising campaign.

Source: The Drayton Bird Partnership

■ How much other door-to-door advertising are you competing with?

This is an important point. Are people going to stare in fascination at your leaflet, wondering whether they've ever seen one of these things before, or will they be clambering over a pile of other leaflets to pick yours up from the mat? In fact, just under a fifth of all household mail is made up of leaflets and coupons, but the proportion varies according to socio-economic group. The following chart shows how many items per household each group averages over a four week period, and what proportion of the total mail it constitutes.

All households		AB households		C1 households		C2 households		DE households	
number of items	%	number of items	%	number of items	%	number of items	%	number of items	%
8.2	22	9.7	20	10.1	24	5.8	18	7.8	25

Source: Direct Mail Information Service, 1994

■ What makes door-to-door advertising effective?

When a leaflet falls through the door, people decide pretty quickly whether to keep it or chuck it. Sometimes they will put information leaflets on one side to read later. How can you maximise the chances of your leaflet being one of the ones they keep?

- People tend to reject anything that seems confusing or complicated.

- They are attracted by money-off coupons, free samples and multi-faceted offers. The more immediate the reward, and the less effort they have to make to get it, the greater is their interest.

- Brand recognition and message or reward must be almost instantaneous.

- Strong, simple visual clues (using colour and shape) work best. Any creative element must be related to either the brand or the reward.

- Any additional product information must be communicated with simplicity.

- People will not usually read detailed copy, so you need to convey the product image through the mood, tone and style of the leaflet.

- Information-style leaflets, such as booklets, should have a feeling of size and quantity of information, and a quality soft-sell approach.

Source: *The Practitioner's Guide to Direct Marketing*, The Institute of Direct Marketing, 1992

■ *How much does the distribution cost?*

You can make a number of savings if you advertise this way, because you don't have to pay for mailing lists, stuffing envelopes or personalising the printing. When it comes to the distribution itself, this tends to be charged per thousand leaflets.

- If you share with other non-competing advertisers (so that your leaflet falls through the door along with three or four others) the costs can be as little as £10–£12 per thousand for a single sheet leaflet.

- Distribution with free newspapers usually costs about the same, or a fraction more.

- Using a distributor who will undertake to deliver your leaflets on their own so they don't have to compete for attention will usually cost from around £25–£30 upwards. You can arrange for all sorts of extras – such as personal calls to prospects – which will obviously add to the cost.

- You need to check that you are using a reputable distributor. It's difficult to check up on them, and some operators can be unreliable.

Source: *The Practitioner's Guide to Direct Marketing*, The Institute of Direct Marketing, 1992

■ *What are the most common complaints about door-to-door advertising?*

You have to be careful not to break the law when it comes to leaflets. Many companies make indiscriminate offers of credit, or quote prices exclusive of VAT and so on. Some people do complain, and you are taking a risk if you don't check with your legal advisers before you finalise the leaflet drop. Here are the most common types of problem in 1993/94.

Prize draws	54%
Itinerant traders (no permanent business address on leaflet)	4%
Slimming/medical/health	6%
Lotteries	1%
Misleading/exaggerated claims	3%
Prices/Consumer Credit Act	27%
Other	5%

Source: Direct Mail Services Standards Board

Free gifts

■ *Do free gifts work?*

The Direct Mail Information Service researched likes and dislikes relating to mailings which included offers of free gifts. It would appear that customers' reactions to free gifts vary tremendously:

Likes	Dislikes
'If you give me a free premium or save me some money somewhere, that is something for nothing.'	'We've all got woks, travel alarm clocks carriage clocks and cheap watches; we don't need any more.'
'If you get something that is a good quality gift, it would be fine.'	'You know it's going to be the cheapest, poorest quality possible version of the thing being offered.'
'It is quite feasible that they are going to give away four CDs, it seems a realistic offer.'	'Every time I've had something like that, I've been bitterly disappointed at the quality of the goods you get.'

Source: *Consumer Creative Benchmarks*, Direct Mail Information Service, 1995

■ *Which business gifts work?*

Gordon Presly, Managing Director of Bemrose Promotional Products, gives two tips:

- When buying business gifts, buyers should not buy what they like – these gifts are not for them. It is what the customer will respond to that counts.

- Calendars and Diaries are still the best value for money promotional products. They are used every day, and their functionality precludes them from ever being received as bribes, unlike other gifts.

Source: *Gordon Presly*, Bemrose Promotional Products

TESTING ADS

■ *What should you test?*

If you never test your ads, you'll never know if you could have got a better response. At its simplest, you test by placing ads that differ in some way, and then comparing the response. Obviously, you need to identify which ad each response came from (print a code on the coupon, for example). Only change one factor between the ads you test, or you won't know which one made the difference. The most common factors to test for are:

- Size of ad
- Position of ad
- Timing of ad
- Product variations
- Price and discounts
- Different response methods
- Different layout, such as a different photo.

Source: The Drayton Bird Partnership

■ *How large a sample should you test?*

The higher the response you expect, the smaller the numbers you need for a valid test result. For example, 500 replies split between two test ads which differ by 10%, would be 95% certain to recur.

Source: The Drayton Bird Partnership

■ *When should you test?*

If you run a test at a time when there is some external factor at work, your results won't be representative. Be very sceptical of test results that are derived during:

- Dramatic news
- Very good weather
- A peak period in your competitors' activity
- Christmas
- Public holidays.

Source: The Drayton Bird Partnership

■ *How soon will your tests yield results?*

It clearly depends on the medium you are testing, and on your business. But you can't plan your campaign fully until you get the results of the tests. So when will that be?

- A daily publication produces quicker results than a weekly; a weekly quicker than a monthly and so on.
- Results build to a peak and then tail off.
- Failures tail off faster than successes.
- Successes build more, and last longer.

Source: The Drayton Bird Partnership

■ *How can you measure the effectiveness of ads that don't ask for a direct response?*

Those last four points were all very helpful – if you're getting phone calls or coupons sent back in reply to your ad. But they don't help much otherwise. What are you supposed to do in these cases? There has been little useful quantitative research in this area, but Raymond Marks of VA Research has years of experience in advertising tracking, and has found that there are two key rules to follow.

1. A single ad on its own will never be as effective as a continued campaign (except if it is in an ongoing reference source such as *Yellow Pages*).
2. Always track your advertising campaigns by asking every lead and enquiry how they heard of you, and use this information to track the effectiveness of your advertising. If you forget to ask contacts how they heard of you, call them back and ask.

Source: Raymond Marks, Managing Director, VA Research

Justifying your advertising spend

■ *How can you justify your advertising spend?*

Many advertising managers could identify with the plaintive cry: 'I know that half the money I spend on advertising is wasted; I just don't know which half.'

In a recent survey, nearly 60% of marketing managers and 80% of agency executives reported that they need to justify their advertising spending now more than they did five years ago.

The Chartered Institute of Marketing has recently pooled the collective wisdom of 190 financial services marketing professionals. Their report provides two sets of lessons:

1 Marketing spending:

- An increased proportion of spending on above-the-line or below-the-line marketing tends to be associated with increased sales.

- Results are clear and statistically significant.

- There was twice the sales response to each £1 of spending below-the-line than there was to spending above-the-line, at least in the short term.

- Sales promotions may increase profit in one situation, but hurt profit in another. The same applies with brand strength and customer retention.

2 Strategy

- How you spend your marketing budget is important; why you spend it is even more so.

- Marketing managers who plan their spending with a focus on brand strength experience increased customer retention for their products.

- Managers who plan their spending with a focus on customer satisfaction are associated with increased product profitability.

- Managers who plan their spending with a focus on new products are associated with increased customer acquisition.

Source: *Value For Money?* The Chartered Institute of Marketing, 1996

CONTENT

Getting your ad seen and read

■ *Will people notice your ad?*

Depressingly few people will even notice a press ad unless you grab their attention.

- Most ads are not seen for longer than two or three seconds.
- Only 20% of readers notice the headline of a small ad.
- Only 1 in 8 of those will read on.

Source: The Drayton Bird Partnership

■ *What factors help to attract attention?*

If those are the facts you're up against, you want to do everything you can to get the reader to spot your ad. Almost invariably, the way to do this is with a good combination of headline and picture. But there are other factors as well, which will pull the reader's eye to your ad.

- People find headlines in capitals and lower case letters much easier to read than headlines that are all in capitals.
- Headlines marooned in the middle of the copy discourage people from reading.
- So do headlines placed under the copy.
- If around half of the ad – or more – is taken up with text, don't put a full stop at the end of the headline. It deters people from reading on.
- Long, unbroken blocks of type are daunting; they can be broken up with crossheads (subheadings within the text), indents and so on.

Sources: The Drayton Bird Partnership and *Communicating or Just Making Pretty Shapes* by Colin Wheildon

Layout and content

■ *Which bits of your ad will people look at first?*

Suppose someone has started reading your ad. The earlier on in the process that they look at each element, the harder that element must work to hold on to them. So it helps to know in what order people scan or read the various components of an ad. Camera tests have indicated that we all tend to read ads in much the same order:

- First, we look at the headline and the picture together.
- Next, we look at the caption.
- Then we look at the bottom right hand corner to see who the advertiser is.
- After that, we start to read the copy. But we may well start in the middle, or read the crossheads first.

Source: The Drayton Bird Partnership

■ *How can you encourage people to keep reading your ad?*

The research findings on readability, on pages 274–281, all apply to designing ads. But one or two other techniques will also encourage people to stay with you for a little longer.

- Headlines should contain enough clear information to stand on their own. Intriguing headlines – unless they contain the message of the ad – may fail.
- Illustrations which block off a column halfway down the page deter the reader from going any further.
- Type set in columns of no more than about 50 characters a line is easy to read.
- Justified text is easier to read.
- More people will read an ad that has a coupon. The bolder the coupon, the higher both the readership and the response are likely to be.

Sources: The Drayton Bird Partnership and *Communicating or Just Making Pretty Shapes* by Colin Wheildon

■ *How can you use the style of the text to keep people reading?*

- The word 'you' should appear 2–3 times more than 'I' or 'we', according to the research of Rudolph Flesch in the 1930s and 1940s.
- Flesch also found that questions which require answers encourage continued reading.
- 'Carrier' words and phrases also keep people hooked. These link one paragraph to the next, for example, 'And there's more...', 'Here's why...' and so on.

Source: The Drayton Bird Partnership

USING ADVERTISING AGENCIES

■ *On what basis do you pay your advertising agency?*

You don't have to pay a straight fee; and many companies don't. One survey of large companies from a cross-section of industries showed that although the most common method of payment is by a straight fee, others are commonly used as well. (A few companies use more than one method of payment, which is why the percentages add up to more than 100.)

Payment for results	3%
Commission/percentage	31%
Straight fees	57%
Payment for ideas	2%
Other	2%
Not stated	15%

Source: Richmond Events Limited

■ *How often should you review your relationship with your ad agency?*

A regular review session with your agency is important to make sure that you're still getting the best out of the relationship, and to identify and iron out any problems or tensions. But what's the norm?

Annually	24%
Every six months	9%
Every quarter	2%
Continually – project by project	12%
No fixed period of time	35%
Not applicable	9%
Not stated	9%

Source: Richmond Events Limited

ADVERTISING

SELLING

CUSTOMERS AND COMPETITORS

Selling to customers

■ *Why do customers buy?*

If you're planning your marketing strategy, or launching a new product or sales initiative, you need the answer to one basic question – what makes a customer purchase your product? Lloyds Bank and the Small Business Research Trust asked 350 small businesses why customers bought their products. The responses revealed that 74% think that a high quality product or service is the reason; the second most important reason was range of products or services (14%).

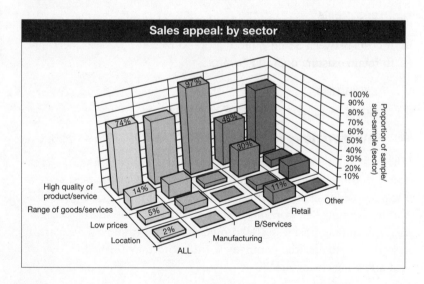

Retailers accept that customers shop around, and only 48% rely mainly on quality and service, with 30% giving emphasis to range of goods and services. Location was a more important consideration in retailing than in other sectors (11%).

Source: *Quarterly Small Business Management Report, Vol. 3, No.4 – Pricing Policies*, Lloyds Bank/Small Business Research Trust, November 1995

■ How much does price influence the decision to buy?

If you're trying to determine your pricing policy, then its important to know how much price matters. Only 5% of respondents overall felt that price was the single most important reason for customer purchases. This varied by sector – 7% in manufacturing, 4% in retailing, but zero in business services.

Source: *Quarterly Small Business Management Report, Vol. 3, No.4 – Pricing Policies*, Lloyds Bank/Small Business Research Trust, November 1995

■ What does it cost to win new customers?

Selling is an expensive business. But selling to new customers is particularly expensive; it usually takes longer, you may have to let them try free samples, you'll probably have to give them brochures, and so on. And at the end of it all, they may still say 'no'. Whereas getting another sale out of an existing customer is far simpler and less costly.

- It costs between 3 and 7 times more to recruit new customers than to retain existing ones.

Source: John Fenton Training International plc

■ How dependent are you on your largest customers?

There is an inherent risk in being over-dependent on a few large customers. You only need to lose one or two and your finances start to look decidedly shaky. If you are in this position are you alone, or is this a common – if worrying – state of affairs? This survey was carried out among businesses who predominantly employed 50 staff or fewer. The smaller the companies, the more they seemed to rely on just a few big customers.

SELLING

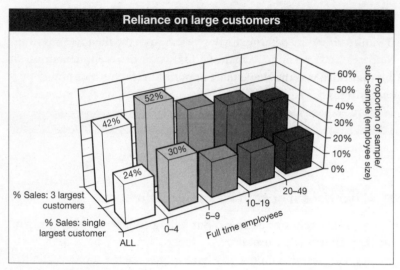

Source: *Quarterly Small Business Management Report 1994 – Customers & Competitors*, Small Business Research Trust

■ Do customers ever say 'no' when they mean 'yes'?

How often have you had customers raise serious objections, only to find that once you have convinced them that they needn't worry on that score, they go ahead and place an order? Sales experts will tell you that an objection is a sign of interest, and that has to be encouraging.

- 73% of customers give 5 or more 'no's before they finally place an order.

Source: John Fenton Training International plc

■ How many times do you have to be told 'no'?

On the basis of the figure above, it seems to be worth hanging on until the buyer runs out of objections. But do you? If you do, you are in the minority.

44% of sales people	quit after the first 'no'
22%	quit after the second 'no'
16%	quit after the third 'no'
10%	quit after the fourth 'no'

That's 92% – leaving just 8% still selling.

Source: John Fenton Training International plc

■ What do buyers dislike most about sales people?

Who better to say what turns buyers off than the buyers themselves? This research was carried out mainly using the membership of the Institute of Purchasing Management as the survey sample. Here is their list:

The top 10 things buyers dislike about sales people
1 They don't know anything about our business.
2 They waste my time.
3 They call too often.
4 They don't call enough.
5 They miss appointments.
6 They break promises.
7 They overclaim.
8 They don't have the authority to negotiate.
9 They don't come to me first.
10 They don't ask for the order.

Source: John Fenton Training International plc

Personal manner

■ When you talk to a customer, how important are the words you use?

We tend to assume that the words are everything in a conversation. But for total communication, tone of voice and body language are far more important. They give you signals and messages that you or your customer may not be aware of consciously, but which are nevertheless vital.

● In a face-to-face selling situation, total communication relies on:

Words	7%
Tone of voice	33%
Body language	60%

SELLING

- When you are teleselling, total communication relies on:

Words   20%
Tone of voice 80%

Source: John Fenton Training International plc

Competitors

■ *How many local competitors do you have?*

Do you find competitors on every street corner, or have you found yourself a niche market? If you feel things are tough going, or if you're thinking of opening a new business or branch, it may help to know how many local competitors it's normal to have. (The respondents in this survey almost all employ fewer than 50 staff.)

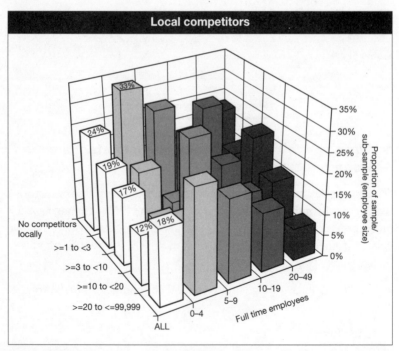

Source: *Quarterly Small Business Management Report 1994 – Customers & Competitors*, Small Business Research Trust

■ *How do you get information about competitors' prices?*

It always helps to know what your competitors are doing. It appears that the most important source of information on competitors' prices is the customers' themselves. A total of 78% of manufacturing firms said that they were informed by customers. Even in retailing, where prices are generally on display, 33% still relied on their customers for information.

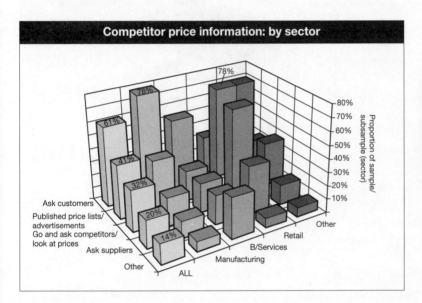

Competitor price information: by sector

SELLING

Retailers and wholesalers also get information from their suppliers (37%). Manufacturers and business service firms use a wider range of methods. Feedback from competitive tendering is relevant here – and many firms use their sales agents to monitor competitors' prices.

Source: Quarterly Small Business Management Report, Vol. 3, No. 4 – Pricing Policies, Lloyds Bank/Small Business Research Trust, November 1995

■ *What are your competitors' strongest points?*

It may be tempting to rubbish the competition, but it's also dangerous. If you don't acknowledge their strengths, how can you challenge them successfully? This survey suggested that the larger the company, the more likely it is to feel that competitors are relatively strong on price. Smaller businesses tend to worry that competitors are more attractive in terms of factors such as range of products, technical support and product appearance.

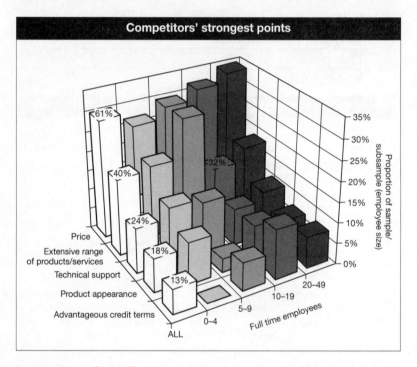

Source: *Quarterly Small Business Management Report 1994* – Customers & Competitors, Small Business Research Trust

RETAILING

■ *What's wrong with service in shops?*

It's very common to hear people complain about 'bad service' in shops, but what exactly do they mean? If you manage a retail outlet or a chain, you need to know what customers object to in order to be sure of eliminating it from your shops. In this survey, consumers were asked which three or four things dissatisfied them most about the service they receive in shops nowadays. The list includes only the factors mentioned by 3% or more of the sample.

Unhelpful/uninterested staff	19%
Long queues at checkouts	19%
Rude/ignorant staff	11%
Poor customer service (slow)	9%
Unknowledgeable staff	8%
High prices/prices increasing	7%
Lack of sales assistants	6%
Poor choice of goods	5%
Staff standing around chatting	5%
Pushy sales assistants	4%
Being pestered by sales staff/not left alone to browse	4%
Lack of personal service	4%
Not enough checkouts open	4%
Unfriendly, miserable staff	3%
Poorly trained staff	3%
Should have a separate till for cheque/credit card payers	3%
Lack of stock/goods out of stock	3%
Keep moving things around/difficult to find things	3%
Poor staff attitude (non-specific)	3%
Problems with staff – any	43%
None/nothing	19%
No answer	6%

Source: *Consumer Concerns 1992*, carried out by MORI for the National Consumer Council. Sample size: 1,978. The field work was carried out between 20 and 24 March 1992.

■ Why do people return goods for an exchange or refund?

When people take goods back to the shop for an exchange or refund, is it generally because they inadvertently bought the wrong size or colour? Or are they returning an unwanted present? Occasionally, of course, it's because the goods are at fault in some way. Respondents in one survey were asked about an occasion in the last 12 months when they had returned goods to the shop where they bought them, and asked the reason why they sought an exchange or refund.

It wasn't the right size/didn't fit properly	32%
Damaged/faulty when bought	27%
Poor quality	10%
Developed fault/broke	8%
It wasn't right colour/style	6%
Unwanted present	6%
Dissatisfied with performance/didn't do what thought	5%
Food past sell by date/off	3%
Product unsafe	1%
Same product cheaper elsewhere	1%
Other	9%
Don't know	1%

So over half the people in this survey returned goods because they were below standard in some way. This suggests that you could substantially reduce returns in shops by improving the quality of the products.

Source: *Consumer Concerns 1992*, carried out by MORI for the National Consumer Council. Sample size: 1,978. The field work was carried out between 20 and 24 March 1992.

■ How willing are shops to give an exchange or refund?

Do you happily give your customers a second chance, or do you resist pressure to give them their money back? Almost a fifth of shops give their customers a hard time. The respondents who answered the last question in this survey were asked: 'When you first returned this product, how willing was the shop to make the exchange/refund?'

Very willing	72%
Fairly willing	9%
Neither willing/unwilling	2%
Fairly unwilling	8%
Very unwilling	9%
Don't know	1%

Source: *Consumer Concerns 1992*, carried out by MORI for the National Consumer Council. Sample size: 1,978. The field work was carried out between 20 and 24 March 1992.

In the end, only 7% of customers in the survey failed to get an exchange or refund; so 10% were getting themselves a reputation for being unhelpful but still ended up giving the customers what they wanted.

■ What do you think is the best way to increase future profits?

As a retailer, you need to know what is the most profitable area for investment in your business. The following chart shows which factors your fellow retailers think will be the most important for future profitability.

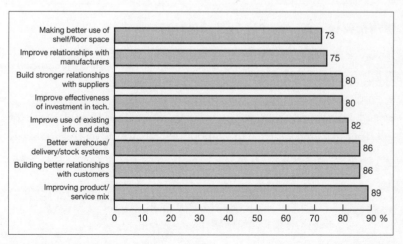

Source: *ICL Retail Survey*, The Henley Centre

FRANCHISING

■ *What is a business format franchise?*

Business format franchise is the granting of a licence by the franchisor to the franchisee, entitling the latter to sell products or services with the aid of a franchise package containing all the elements necessary to establish a business and run it profitably in an established routine. This should cover the following points:

● eliminate as far as possible the risks inherent in setting up a new business – the package's success should already have been proved through a market-tested pilot operation

● enable a person to be their own boss to establish a business of pre-designed format, with full support of the franchisor

● set out in detail in operations manual precisely how the business should be run

● have an easily identifiable, eye-catching brand image with growing public awareness.

Source: *The Two Partners of Franchising*, Peter Stern, Franchise World Directory, 1998

■ *How widespread is franchising?*

If you're thinking of getting into franchising, it's woth knowing how mainstream it is nowadays.

● Annual sales relating to franchising in the UK now total £6.4bn.

● 541 business-format franchisors have created 26,800 separate businesses, and more than 264,000 people are currently employed in franchising

● 94% of franchisees claim profitability.

Source: *1997 NatWest/BFA Franchise Survey*, NatWest UK and the British Franchise Association

■ What characteristics do franchisors look for in franchisees?

What do the experts think are the most important characteristics for success in a prospective franchisee? Franchisors increasingly do not specify any age or gender preferences for potential franchisees, but experience and, especially, attitude were considered important. Here's the percentage of franchisors who thought the following aspects mattered:

Characteristics for success	All franchisors		
	1994	1995	1996
Experience			
Selling and marketing	32%	42%	51%
Other aspects of business	27%	30%	45%
This industry	24%	19%	28%
Self employment	17%	16%	25%
Don't specify	39%	41%	28%
Attitude			
Self motivated	88%	98%	95%
Financially aware	73%	86%	84%
Hard worker	84%	91%	91%
Hands on/owner operator	69%	77%	73%
Don't specify	4%	1%	4%

Source: *NatWest*/BFA Franchise Survey, 1997

■ What sort of educational qualifications do franchisees have?

If you're thinking of starting up a franchise business, or you're interviewing potential franchisees, how important are educational qualifications to success? Only 22% of franchisees have no qualifications at all, while 17% hold university degrees. Generally speaking, the trend is towards better educated franchisees.

Qualifications	All franchisees		
	1994	1995	1996
None	15%	18%	22%
GCSE/CSE/O level	24%	23%	19%
A level	11%	8%	12%
City and Guilds/trade	16%	16%	17%
OND/HND/Diploma	13%	19%	10%
Degree	20%	14%	17%
MBA	1%	2%	2%

Source: NatWest/BFA Franchise Survey, 1997

■ *What quality of relationship do franchisees have with their franchisors?*

This is a crucial ingredient in a successful and stress-free franchise operation. An encouraging 92% of franchisees consider their relationship with their franchisor to be at least mainly satisfactory; what's more, this figure is gradually on the increase.

Quality of relationship	All franchisees		
	1994	1995	1996
Definitely satisfactory	44%	47%	55%
Mainly satisfactory	46%	39%	37%
TOTAL SATISFACTORY	**90%**	**86%**	**92%**
Mainly not satisfactory	7%	7%	4%
Definitely not satisfactory	3%	7%	5%
TOTAL UNSATISFACTORY	**10%**	**14%**	**9%**

Source: NatWest/BFA Franchise Survey, 1997

■ How often should you review your franchise agreement?

If you want to remain competitive, and keep pace with changing markets, you need to keep the key functions of your business under constant review. For franchisors, this must include their standard franchise agreement. Franchisors were asked when, if ever, they last had a major review of their franchise agreement.

Time of last review	All franchisors	
	1995	1996
Never/no major review	18%	23%
Within the last year	52%	49%
1–2 years ago	15%	18%
3–5 years ago	7%	7%
6+ years ago	2%	1%
Don't know	6%	1%

Source: NatWest/BFA Franchise Survey, 1997

■ Are franchisees likely to renew their contracts?

One of the best measures of success is whether, when the contract expires, the franchisee wants to come back for more. Those franchisees with three years or less of their contract to run were asked whether or not they wished to renew.

Franchisees' wishes	1995	1996
Wish to renew	72%	77%
Do not wish to renew	8%	6%
Undecided	20%	16%

- 25% of franchisors report that they charge a fee for contract renewal, a figure which has steadily decreased since 1991 (22%).

Source: NatWest/BFA Franchise Survey, 1997

The Franchisor

■ *What are the advantages to the franchisor?*

If you are considering taking a franchise, what are the benefits?

- The system gives franchisors the ability to expand an existing successful business more rapidly than by using their own capital.
- Day-to-day administrative/staffing problems sometimes associated with company-owned chains are greatly reduced.
- The franchisor gains wider buying opportunities, and is in a better position to acquire national accounts.

Source: *The Two Partners of Franchising*, Peter Stern, Franchise World Directory, 1998

■ *What are the drawbacks to the franchisor?*

This sounds so rosy – but there have to be drawbacks. What are they? Standards of product and service have to be maintained – if one outlet fails, it can do irreparable damage to the whole. Communications may become a problem. The secret of success is to select franchisees with care.

Source: *The Two Partners of Franchising*, Peter Stern, Franchise World Directory, 1998

■ *What factors should a prospective franchisor consider?*

The franchisor's 8 key factors
1 Is there sufficiently wide-scale market demand?
2 Is the product/service competitive and franchisable?
3 What, if any, is the competition?
4 Has the product staying power, or is it a passing fad?
5 Can a distinctive attractive image be created?
6 Can a simple framework be established?
7 Can effective controls be established?
8 Is there sufficient depth of management to recruit franchisees and to lead and develop the franchise?

If the answers are all positive, then at least one pilot scheme should be launched and run for at least 12 months. In many cases, it would be wiser to run several pilot schemes in tandem for a longer period.

Source: *The Two Partners of Franchising*, Peter Stern, Franchise World Directory, 1998

■ What preparations do you need to make for a successful franchise?

- A well written prospectus
- Protection of intellectual property rights through registered trademarks and copyrights
- Drawing up of a franchise contract to include licensing, terms, fees, rights and advertising policy.

Source: *The Two Partners of Franchising*, Peter Stern, Franchise World Directory, 1998

■ How much will it cost to establish a franchise?

To get to break-even stage might take £75,000–£100,000; a major operator might exceed £250,000.

Source: *The Two Partners of Franchising*, Peter Stern, Franchise World Directory, 1998

■ How can a franchisor expand abroad?

There are several options:

- Direct franchising
- Establishing a subsidiary in each country which then sells franchises
- Expansion via company-owned outlets
- Sale of a national or regional licence to someone abroad, allowing that person to develop the franchise.

This fourth option is the most popular. The franchise should always be pilot tested in each new country.

Source: *The Two Partners of Franchising*, Peter Stern, Franchise World Directory, 1998

SELLING

The Franchisee

■ What are the advantages of franchising for the franchisee?

10 advantages for the franchisee

1 Proven business know-how of the franchisor
2 Established brand-names
3 Large-scale advertising of brand-name and business
4 Training on product and business skills
5 Full support during start-up
6 Detailed operations manual
7 Ongoing advice and guidance
8 Agreed area of operation
9 Rights and obligations clearly defined
10 Commitment by franchisor to maximise franchisee's development – because their income depends on it

Source: *The Two Partners of Franchising*, Peter Stern, Franchise World Directory, 1998

■ What should you check about a franchise?

If you are considering a franchise, what should you look out for? Are there ways of checking the soundness of the investment? Look carefully at:

• The business track record
• The management and franchise experience of its principals
• The total cash input, including working capital.

Source: *The Two Partners of Franchising*, Peter Stern, Franchise World Directory, 1998

■ What should potential franchisees avoid?

Any of these might indicate danger:

• The hard sell
• A heavy initial franchise fee
• The absence of a pilot operation
• Pyramid selling.

Source: *The Two Partners of Franchising*, Peter Stern, Franchise World Directory, 1998

■ *Do failure rates vary by sector?*

The simple answer is yes. Health care seems a stable option. Over an 11 year period, surveying 1,658 franchising firms, only 25% of health care firms had ceased franchising. The same survey recorded a wide difference in failure rates in other sectors.

Sector	Failure rate, 1984–95
Health care	25%
Print and publishing	41%
Hotel and catering	57%
Miscellaneous sector	93%

Source: Behind the Veneer of Success: Propensities for UK Franchisor Failure, Small Business Research Trust, 1997

Costs and profits

■ *How much does it cost to set up a franchise operation?*

If you want to take on a franchise, you'll need some idea of the capital outlay, and where the money goes. The NatWest/BFA survey asked franchisors which initial charges they made, and recorded what proportion of them made each type of charge.

Franchise fee	94%
Equipment	70%
Stock	55%
Working capital	77%

- The survey established that the average initial outlay for a franchisee was £40,200.

Source: NatWest/BFA Franchise Survey, 1997

■ What are the ongoing costs involved in running a franchise?

Once you've paid the set-up costs, you still have to pay the franchisor a percentage of your turnover as an ongoing charge. Again, franchisors were asked which ongoing charges they made.

Management services fee	73%
Advertising contribution	61%
Mark-up	43%
Other	39%

N.B. Mark-up is adjusted to represent mark-up on ultimate sale value.

● The survey found the average ongoing charge payable to the franchisor was 11.1%.

Source: *NatWest/BFA* Franchise Survey, 1997

■ How profitable is a franchise operation for the franchisee?

Before you get involved in franchising, you need to know how profitable it's likely to be. If you're already franchising, you'll want to know if your performance compares respectably with that of other

Performance	All franchisees			
	1993	1994	1995	1996
Highly profitable	10%	5%	5%	11%
Quite profitable	33%	47%	37%	47%
Marginally profitable	44%	35%	48%	36%
TOTAL PROFITABLE	**87%**	**87%**	**90%**	**94%**
Just loss making	8%	10%	6%	4%
Definitely loss making	5%	3%	4%	2%
TOTAL LOSS MAKING	**13%**	**13%**	**10%**	**6%**

franchisees. The survey asked franchisees to report on their own performance. There has been an encouraging growth in profitability over the last six years – in 1991, only 70% were profitable.

Source: *NatWest/BFA* Franchise Survey, 1994

EXPORTING

■ *Who do you rely on for expertise in conducting your business abroad?*

If you do a lot of business abroad, you will doubtless have some kind of in-house expertise. But suppose you don't have much overseas trade, or you're just starting out, or entering a new market or activity. Where can you go for advice?

The majority of those who currently export (61%) seek advice on exporting issues. The most popular sources of advice are Government departments and Chambers of Commerce. Business support organisations include Training and Enterprise Councils and Business Link.

Sources of advice	
DTI/British Overseas Trade Board	23%
Chambers of Commerce	21%
Business colleagues/family/friends	15%
Business support organisations	4%
Trade associations	3%
Banks/building societies	1%

Source: *Realising your Export Potential*, Barclays Bank plc Small Business Services, 1996

■ *How much research is necessary?*

Researching a market is an essential part of running a successful business. Yet it would appear that few exporters research their overseas market. Only 1 in 5 carry out any research prior to exporting; 1% seek professional help.

Research carried out prior to exporting	
None	80%
Desk research	10%
Field research by business or UK-based employer	10%
Field research undertaken by overseas agents	4%
Specialist research company	1%
Government market information enquiry service	1%
Other	2%

Source: *Realising your Export Potential*, Barclays Bank plc Small Business Services, 1996

■ *What topics are usually researched?*

When businesses do undertake research, it tends to be into activities which will have a direct impact on sales, such as product and market accessiblity.

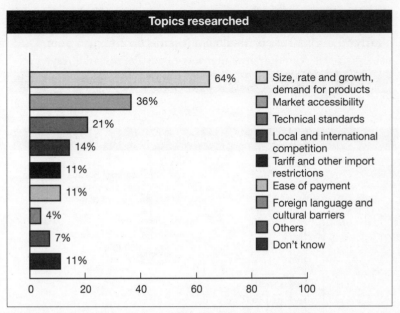

Topics researched

64%	☐ Size, rate and growth, demand for products
36%	▨ Market accessibility
21%	■ Technical standards
14%	■ Local and international competition
11%	■ Tariff and other import restrictions
11%	▨ Ease of payment
4%	▨ Foreign language and cultural barriers
7%	▨ Others
11%	■ Don't know

Source: *Realising your Export Potential*, Barclays Bank plc Small Business Services, 1996

SELLING

■ *Do you need specific training for exporting?*

Nearly three-quarters of exporters have never undertaken specific training. Where they have, it usually focuses on finance and marketing skills. If you're not a gifted linguist, don't worry – languages do not figure high on the list.

Training undertaken	Percentage
None	74%
Export finance	11%
Marketing and promotion	10%
Law	7%
Export documentation	5%
Languages	3%
Distribution/transport	1%
Other	1%

Source: *Realising your Export Potential*, Barclays Bank plc Small Business Services, 1996

■ *Is training really necessary?*

Nearly 9 out of 10 exporters do not feel it is necessary to train.

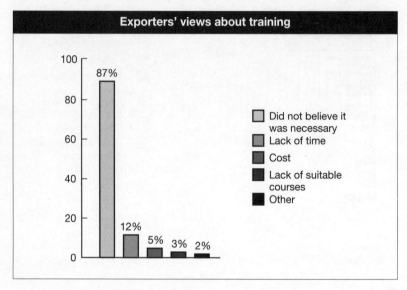

Source: *Realising your Export Potential*, Barclays Bank plc Small Business Services, 1996

■ *What are the greatest barriers to overseas business?*

Many business people hold out against doing business overseas because they don't have a clue how to go about it. Fear of the unknown is a significant barrier for 45% of businesses with fewer than 100 employees. One of the best ways to counter this is to know what you're up against, and then you can prepare. The following chart shows the factors that respondents considered to be the greatest barriers.

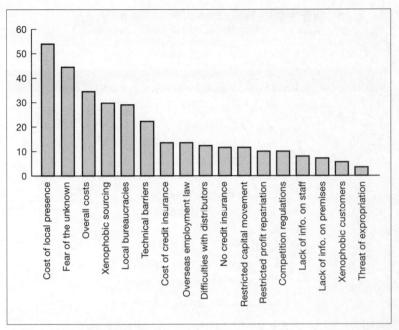

Source: *Internationalisation for World Class Business Strategies*, Association of British Chambers of Commerce, 1995

■ How do you go about choosing an overseas agent or distributor?

If you decide to sell overseas through a third party, you are putting your future success in the region into their hands. But are they safe hands? The best (and most popular) way to find an agent or distributor is by personal recommendation, but this isn't always available. So if you're investigating or interviewing several agents or distributors, what are the most important qualifications they should possess? The following table shows how one sample of UK exporters said they ranked the key criteria for selecting agents and distributors.

The top 14 criteria for selecting agents

1 Knowledge of market
2 Market coverage
3 Enthusiasm for the product
4 Knowledge of the product
5 Good reputation
6 Number and quality of sales staff
7 Previous success
8 Good connections
9 Frequency of sales calls
10 Service and stocking facilities
11 Costs involved
12 Quality of service staff
13 Dealings with competitors
14 Executive career histories

Source: *A Profile of UK Exporting Companies – An Empirical Study*, by Richard A Moore, from *Journal of Marketing Management*

Why export?

■ *Why not?*

Most businesses in the UK with a turnover of up to £10 million currently do not export their products or services. A large majority (83%) of them have never considered doing so.

Source: *Realising your Export Potential*, Barclays Bank plc Small Business Services, 1996

■ *Why are many businesses reluctant to export?*

Many businesses see their products as unsuitable for an overseas market. Other concerns about exporting are not ranked as highly.

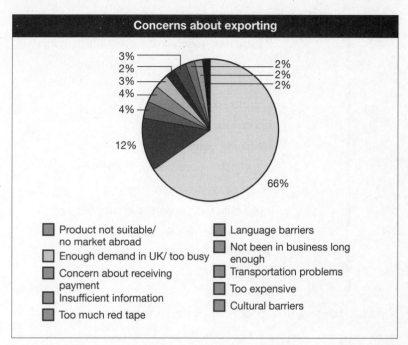

Concerns about exporting

- Product not suitable/ no market abroad
- Enough demand in UK/ too busy
- Concern about receiving payment
- Insufficient information
- Too much red tape
- Language barriers
- Not been in business long enough
- Transportation problems
- Too expensive
- Cultural barriers

Source: *Realising your Export Potential*, Barclays Bank plc Small Business Services, 1996

■ *What are the most common reasons for starting to export?*

Why should you export? Why not just sit at home and carry on as you always have? If you're just considering going into exports, you might find it useful to know why other people make this decision. This part of the survey was about overseas business in general. About a quarter of the respondents were involved in importing, either as well as exporting, or without exporting at all. The following results reflect this.

Very important   Expansion into new markets

Personal experience of a particular country

Visit overseas by a director or manager of the business

Personal contacts

Improving quality

Reducing costs

Approach from a potential customer

Word of mouth opportunity

Approach from a potential supplier

Unsolicited overseas order

Reaction to competitor moves

Suggestion from government or trade organisation

Not at all important   Strategy of vertical integration

Source: *Internationalisation for World Class Business Strategies*, Association of British Chambers of Commerce, 1995

■ *Is your business too small to export?*

Ian Fletcher, Senior Policy Adviser at the BCC (British Chambers of Commerce), has the following tips for a first time exporter.

> *Many of the factors which make a business successful at home are equally applicable when trading abroad. Size itself should not be a barrier. If you have a good quality product or service, the capacity to deal with additional orders, and sound financial management, you are halfway towards becoming a successful exporter.*

He gives his top eight tips for exporters.

Top 8 tips for exporters
1 Look before you leap – research your market thoroughly
2 Consider how you will trade abroad – directly? agent? distributor?
3 Make sure you retain control of how your product will be marketed
4 Contracts are crucial. Do not release goods until the contract defining payment is signed
5 Consider what you will do if you do not get paid
6 Ensure that export documentation is thoroughly checked and meets specific country requirements
7 Build into your prices the cost of credit and any exchange rate risk
8 Take it slowly. Do not spread your resources too thinly

Source: Ian Fletcher, Senior Policy Adviser, British Chambers of Commerce

SELLING

■ What makes small business exports fail?

Exporting requires hard work. It can expose cruelly poor business planning. The British Chambers of Commerce asked a selection of small firms what had led to their export failures. The two most popular responses were:

- 45% put insufficient time/resources into the failed venture
- 30% did insufficient research/preparatory work.

Source: *Small Firms Survey – Exporting*, British Chambers of Commerce, May 1997

■ Do you need to speak the same language?

The language barrier appears to be minimal. English is considered by 1 in 3 exporters as the international business language. Only 1 in 5 businesses feels it is necessary to use the services of a translator or interpreter – usually when trading with South America, Africa, Asia and the Far East.

Source: *Realising your Export Potential*, Barclays Bank plc Small Business Services, 1996

■ *Which marketing activities promote exports?*

Translated brochures and other promotional literature are used by about half of exporters, as are advertising and direct marketing. The costs associated with travel and distribution dissuade many exporters from visiting their customers abroad or sending samples before contracts are signed.

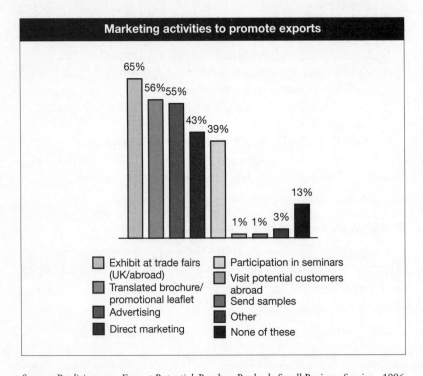

Marketing activities to promote exports

65%
56% 55%
43%
39%
13%
1% 1% 3%

☐ Exhibit at trade fairs (UK/abroad)
☐ Translated brochure/ promotional leaflet
☐ Advertising
■ Direct marketing
☐ Participation in seminars
☐ Visit potential customers abroad
☐ Send samples
■ Other
■ None of these

Source: *Realising your Export Potential*, Barclays Bank plc Small Business Services, 1996

■ *How do you find out about overseas business opportunities?*

For all you know, there are customers in Portugal or Peru just crying out for your product. So how can you find out who – and where – they are? The following chart shows where other businesses go to gather information about overseas business opportunities.

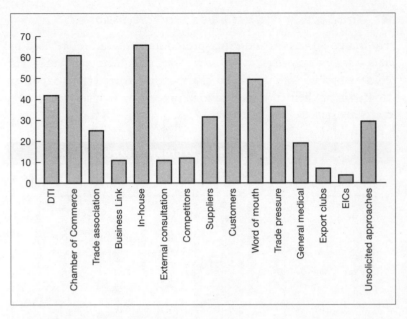

Source: *Internationalisation for World Class Business Strategies*, Association of British Chambers of Commerce, 1995

■ Which regulatory factors influence your decision on which countries to do business with?

Sometimes you may move into a particular foreign market for a specific reason – perhaps you know the area, or an agent has approached you asking to sell your products there. But if you have a more generalised wish to expand overseas, how do you decide which country to do business in? Among the most important factors to take into account are the regulatory factors, such as trade barriers. The following chart shows which ones businesses take into account when selecting a suitable country to trade in.

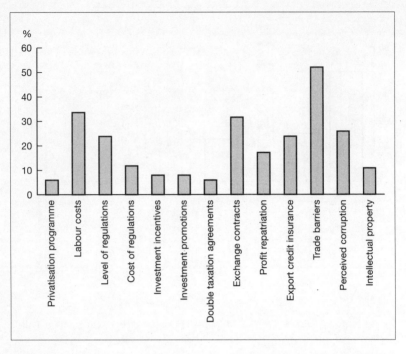

Source: Internationalisation for World Class Business Strategies, Association of British Chambers of Commerce, 1995

■ *Which other factors influence your decision?*

Once you've checked out the regulatory factors, there are other things you will want to consider as well. Is the country in question on the verge of a military coup, for example? Or is it physically inaccessible? The following chart shows how many businesses in the survey took each factor into account.

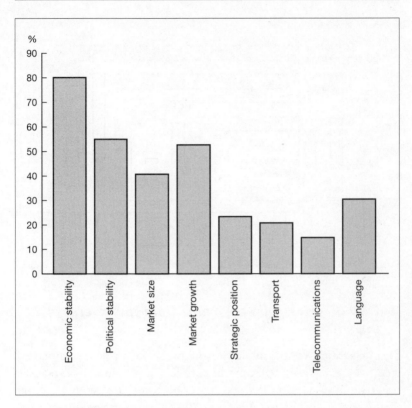

Source: *Internationalisation for World Class Business Strategies*, Association of British Chambers of Commerce, 1995

Credit control

■ *How do you assess the creditworthiness of new overseas customers?*

Some businesses avoid the need to check their customers' creditworthiness by using letters of credit, or they use credit insurance agencies or factoring companies. But if you don't go for these options, how can you be sure that they'll pay up? The following chart shows how one survey's respondents check on their new overseas buyers.

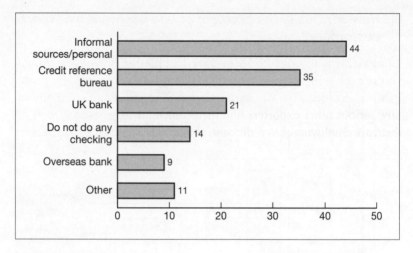

Source: *Royal Bank of Scotland Quarterly Survey of Exporters*, Small Business Research Trust, June 1995

■ *How do you ensure payments from your overseas buyers?*

Even assuming you've made thorough checks on your customers' creditworthiness, you still can't be sure they'll pay up unless you take other steps. What do other exporters do to ensure payments from their overseas customers? A total of 70% of them in this survey do at least some business with no formal method of protection at all (see the following chart).

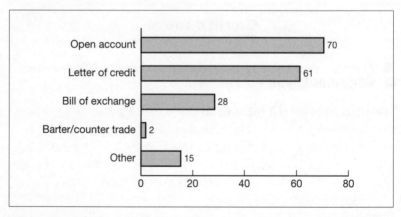

Source: *Royal Bank of Scotland Quarterly Survey of Exporters*, Small Business Research Trust, June 1995

■ How serious is the problem of late payment by export customers?

Late payment of course can be catastrophic for businesses. But if you're exporting, do you tend to find ways of avoiding these problems, or do they give you serious grief? The following chart shows how serious other exporters find the problem; it suggests that most of them are employing the credit control methods above to good effect.

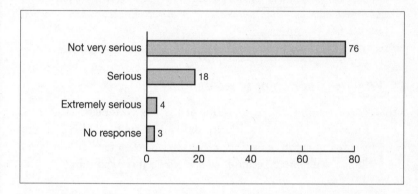

Source: *Royal Bank of Scotland Quarterly Survey of Exporters*, Small Business Research Trust, June 1995

EXHIBITING

■ Why should you exhibit?

Bill Richards of the Exhibition Industry Federation provided the following advice.

> *Why exhibit? The simple answer has to be 'to win friends and influence people'. The more considered approach has to be related to the product or service that you are promoting. Prospective clients can see it, even play with it, and talk to people who really know about it. Exhibitions are industry sector related; they are an opportunity to meet and get to*

know the buyers and suppliers in that sector, thus they are already targeted at a market.

Since they are so specifically targeted, they represent value for money in promotional and sales terms. First time exhibitors should not exhibit at an exhibition that they have not previously visited – learn the territory. You can make contact with more sales prospects in the 2–3 days of a trade exhibition than in several months of direct sales calls.

Use the exhibition as an opportunity to gather information, personal and business, collect and qualify contact addresses and new supplier data, and then follow up – this will make your direct sales calls more personal and specific.'

Source: *Bill Richards*, Exhibition Industry Federation

■ Why do other companies exhibit?

Why do you exhibit? There are a lot of reasons you might choose to, as the following table shows. It's not only interesting but also useful to see why other companies exhibit; it could give you a few ideas beyond the standard 'we're here because we always do this exhibition'.

Objective	Percentage importance			
	Very	Fairly	Somewhat	Not
Launch new products	35	24	19	20
Sell directly	25	22	20	30
Make presence felt	70	21	6	3
Demonstrate products	26	27	19	26
New sales prospects	83	10	5	1
Test new ideas	6	12	21	59
Media coverage	14	28	29	25
Market research	4	18	30	46
New agents	19	20	14	44

Source: *Effectiveness Survey*, Exhibition Industry Federation

■ Are exhibitions an effective marketing medium?

Obviously exhibitions are an important part of the marketing mix for many companies, and a fairly expensive one at that. So are they worth it? We'll look at the costs later on, but in general, how do companies feel their effectiveness compares with other major marketing activities? They seem to score pretty highly, although it's worth remembering that this was a survey of exhibitors, so you wouldn't expect many of them to give exhibitions a very low rating (although 2% of respondents did; it makes you wonder why they do it).

Medium	Percentage effectiveness			
	Very	Fairly	Somewhat	Not
Exhibitions	17	46	16	2
Advertising	15	37	17	8
Direct mail	15	27	13	6
Other	13	17	8	4

Source: *Effectiveness Survey*, Exhibition Industry Federation

■ How useful are exhibitions for launching new products?

We've already seen that 35% of respondents in one survey considered exhibitions 'very important' for launching new products. But you can launch a new product through more than one medium. So how do these exhibitors think that exhibitions compare with other media when it comes to new product launches?

Medium	Rated best by
Trade press	32%
Trade exhibitions	23%
Direct mail	10%
Newspapers	7%
Public Relations	7%
Sales reps	4%
TV	3%
Conferences/seminars	2%
Radio	1%
Don't know	11%

Source: *Effectiveness Survey*, Exhibition Industry Federation

SELLING

■ *For a successful exhibition, what are the most important things to plan?*

No one who has ever exhibited needs telling that there are plenty of things that can go wrong. The problem is, you're never quite sure what all of them are. That's why they go wrong. All too often, the real problem is that there is so much to remember that you're almost bound to forget something. What would really help is a checklist of all the most important things to do, drawn up by an expert, that includes all the things that can so easily get forgotten. And here it is:

Checklist for exhibitors
1 Application for space
2 Payment of deposit
3 Stand design
4 Lighting plan
5 Order lighting
6 Order water, drainage, gas, if required
7 Order heating, power as required
8 Check use of fire hazard materials in stand construction
9 Order fire extinguishers
10 Insurance for stand and exhibits
11 Organise products to be exhibited
12 Arrangements for special delivery of large, heavy products
13 Order stand furniture, ashtrays etc.
14 Organise flooring, covering
15 Night sheets
16 Order telephone service for exhibition period (mobiles may not function well in buildings with a high steel content)
17 Contract for stand cleaning
18 Arrange for photography
19 Stand models, staffing of stand
20 Order flowers for stand
21 Hotel accommodation

22 Office accessories and stationery to use on stand
23 Design and prepare handouts/literature
24 Order any special lettering for displays
25 Prepare press releases
26 Description and price cards for exhibits
27 Order drinks for stand
28 Invitations to customers and prospects
29 Security, especially night before opening
30 Stand personnel training, duties, daily rotas, free time etc.

Source: John Fenton Training International plc

SELLING

■ How do you make a record of who visits the stand?

Apart from any selling you do directly from your stand, your presence at an exhibition is almost worthless unless you come away with a list of good contacts to follow up and sell to later. So how do you collect this information? Enquiry forms seem to be the most popular way, and some exhibitors use more than one method:

Enquiry forms	71%
Business cards	47%
Tracking forms	24%
Brochures	20%

Source: Exhibition Industry Federation

■ How long does it take to convert exhibition enquiries into sales?

Are you expecting to call up all your contacts as soon as you get back to the office and get an order out of them, or will it take years of wooing them before you finally clinch a sale? Obviously it will vary to some extent from business to business. But if you're going to plan, budget and cost your exhibition attendances properly, you'll need to know roughly how long it takes. And to do that, you'll need to be able to link the sale to the original exhibition enquiry.

- The average time to convert a sales lead for respondents to this survey was seven months, although in a number of cases the lead time was two years or more.
- Just over half the exhibitors sampled could specifically identify exhibition leads.

Source: Exhibition Industry Federation

Costs

■ *What proportion of your marketing budget goes on exhibitions?*

Exhibitions are expensive, but many regular exhibitors clearly find them well worth it, or they wouldn't keep attending them. But how much of your budget do they take up? Here's the proportion of their marketing budgets that respondents spent on exhibitions so, for example, 6% of them spend under 10% on exhibitions.

% Budget	% Respondents
0–9	6
10–19	10
20–29	21
30–39	9
40–49	12
50–59	15
60–69	7
over 70%	14

Source: Exhibition Industry Federation

■ *What is your annual exhibitions budget?*

We've established that exhibitions aren't cheap, but just how expensive are they? If your organisation gets a lot of business through exhibitions, how much should you expect to spend each year? Here are the 1993 figures for the average amount spent by organisations on exhibitions during the year, broken down by size of organisation. (Remember 1993 was a recession year, but these figures are useful nonetheless, and are the most up to date available.)

No. of employees	£ spent per year
Under 50	16,100
50–99	30,100
100–499	65,400
500–999	28,200
1,000–4,999	127,300
5,000 or more	80,100
Average spend	30,500

Source: Exhibition Industry Federation

■ *Where does the money go?*

So what are you spending this average of over £30,000 on? The three main areas you need to cover are stand/stand space, staff and promotion. Here's a breakdown of how the total is made up from these three areas of spending.

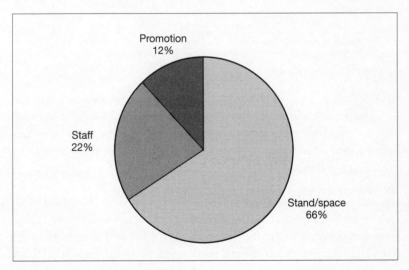

Source: Exhibition Industry Federation

Exhibition visitors

■ *Why do people visit exhibitions?*

If you don't know why the visitors are attending the exhibition, you can't hope to give them what they want. Buyers find exhibitions useful because they provide face-to-face contact with suppliers, they give them the chance to see product demonstrations, and they give them an opportunity to make product comparisons.

- 89% of respondents said that the opportunity to make face-to-face contacts was important or very important.
- 87% said that demonstration of products was important or very important.
- 77% said that the ability to compare products was important or very important.

When it comes to the single most important reason for visiting exhibitions, the visitors in this survey gave the following responses:

Keep abreast of technology	35%
To see what is new generally	25%
To see new products and meet existing suppliers	14%
To see new products and meet new suppliers	12%
Other reasons	14%

Source: Exhibition Industry Federation

- Another survey, this time conducted among members of the Chartered Institute of Purchasing and Supply, found that more than half the respondents use exhibitions as a source of information, and 6% find exhibitions the single most important way of sourcing supplier markets.

Source: Chartered Institute of Purchasing and Supply, 1994

■ What action do people take as a result of visiting exhibitions?

Do buyers simply enjoy the day out and then go back to what they were doing before, or do their visits to exhibitions actually change the way they do things? The following findings come from a survey of large companies from a cross-section of industries, who were surveyed about a specific marketing exhibition. Although some of the answers are marketing related, many of them are likely to be indicative of the general approach among buyers who visit exhibitions. The respondents were asked what action they were likely to take as a result of attending the exhibition. It looks as if most of them have a busy time ahead.

Arrange further meetings with exhibitors	81%
Implement new initiatives	61%
Make/recommend specific amendments to our marketing strategy	54%
View potential new service suppliers in a different light	50%
Request further information from exhibitors	43%
Look at new media channels/activities	39%
Review our relationships with current service suppliers	22%
Review our budget spend	13%
Other	1%

Source: Richmond Events Limited, 1995

Advice

■ How can you guarantee that your stand attracts people?

The object of 'attracting' people to your stand is to register them as useful sales contacts. This means that you want only serious enquiries from potential customers who warm to you. Bill Richards of the Exhibition Industry Federation has the following tips.

Top 6 tips for exhibitors

1 Train your staff to welcome – not to defend the stand from marauders
2 Try to achieve a good position
3 Use visual techniques to engage the visitor's interest – good design, eye-catching movement, on-the-stand interactivity
4 Arrange a competition
5 Distribute leaflets to encourage competitors to visit your stand
6 Make the prize an intriguing – or universally welcome – one, and the competition fun

Source: *Bill Richards*, Exhibition Industry Federation

PRESENTATIONS

■ *What are the most common mistakes people make when giving a presentation?*

You can – and should – rehearse your presentation until you know it backwards. But when your big moment comes, you can't concentrate on everything at once. So what are the key mistakes to avoid? Surveys into presentation techniques and practices are somewhat thin on the ground. However, the experience of people who work in the field is at least as helpful. Khalid Aziz formed The Aziz Corporation in the early 1980s to help people improve their spoken communications. Training in presentation skills is obviously a large part of this. So here, courtesy of Khalid Aziz, are the five most common mistakes:

The 5 most common mistakes

1 Failure to understand and relate to the audience
2 Using overhead projector slides as notes on screen for you rather than as visual aids for the audience
3 Failure to use eye contact, particularly on points of passion
4 Looking at the screen rather than the audience
5 Trying to read from hand-written notes which are far too detailed

Source: The Aziz Corporation

■ What are the key factors for a successful presentation?

Presentations can be nerve-racking for many people. But if you know what makes them successful, and put it into practice, you need never be nervous again. Here are Khalid Aziz's five key factors for successful presentations:

The 5 key factors for successful presentations

1 Allow enough time for preparation and rehearsal
2 Consult with colleagues about the type of people in the target audience
3 Distil notes on to cards, clearly printed in block capitals
4 Rehearse – including visual aids – in front of colleagues for constructive feedback
5 Make sure there is a clear 'call to action' in your presentation, so the audience can do something in your favour as a result of your presentation

Source: The Aziz Corporation

■ How can you judge how long your presentation will be?

Of course you will practise your presentation before you give it. But when you're at the writing stage, a good rule of thumb to follow is that it will take four to five times as long to speak as it does to read to yourself in your head:

- A television newsreader reads aloud at 3 words per second.
- Educated people can read print in their head at up to 15 words per second.

Source: The Aziz Corporation

■ What should you put on an overhead projector slide?

A useful touchstone for deciding whether to include a particular slide in your presentation is the 'necessary and sufficient' rule:

- The information on the slide must be necessary, and the total set of slides should be sufficient, or the slide should not be there.

Visual aids are not notes on screen for you to use, as we have already seen. But it is sometimes helpful to use verbal overheads. Here's a useful guide if you do use words on your slides:

- No more than five words per line
- No more than five lines per slide.

Source: The Aziz Corporation

■ How detailed should your notes be?

We've already seen that your prompt cards shouldn't be too detailed. But what is too detailed? The same rule of thumb that applies to overhead slides is also useful here. Each prompt card should have:

- No more than five words per line
- No more than five lines per card.

Source: The Aziz Corporation

CUSTOMER CARE

MANAGING CUSTOMER CARE

Planning a customer care programme

■ *How do you plan a good customer care programme?*

If you don't have a customer care programme, do you want to know where to start? MSB – Managing the Service Business – focus on service standards. They maintain that there are four key elements to good customer service:

1 **Market research** – focuses research to establish markets and customers
2 **Consultancy** – to build the strategy and encourage positive relationships
3 **Communication** – to make sure that customers receive consistent messages from your business
4 **Training** – to make sure that all staff are involved in customer care, and committed to continuous improvement of standards.

Source: *Improving Business Performance Through Service Excellence*, MSB, 1997

Setting up a customer care programme

■ *Who should take responsibility for customer care?*

Whose job is it in your company? Perhaps the board of directors? Or senior management? If you run into problems with setting up or running a customer care programme, it might help to know what other companies do. The following survey asked managers who in the organisation was responsible, and then went on to ask who the respondents believed *should* have responsibility. The results show clearly that respondents feel that everyone should share the load.

Responsible person/department	Has primary responsibility	Should have responsibility
Board of directors/top policy committee	21%	23%
Chief executive/managing director	21%	16%
Senior management	16%	8%
Line managers	9%	4%
Supervisors	1%	–
Personnel/human resources department	1%	1%
Customer service department	7%	1%
All employees	21%	45%
Other	2%	2%
Don't know	2%	–

Source: *Raising the Standard – A Survey of Managers' Attitudes to Customer Care*, Institute of Management

■ *Does a formal investment in customer care make a difference?*

If you're introducing a customer care programme, you can adopt a fairly low-key approach: introduce useful measures bit by bit, hold a few training sessions, and generally raise the standard without making a big thing out of it. Or you can adopt a more formal approach: announce the programme, plan and schedule the intended measures, arrange training programmes and even invest in new technology to help improve your customer care standards.

Formal programmes

- Almost 60% of organisations in this survey had introduced a formal customer care programme (only 13% had had one in place for more than three years).

- In organisations which had recently launched a formal customer care programme, more than 90% of managers felt that this had improved customer care.

- 71% of larger companies (over 5,000 employees) have formal customer care programmes in place; 40% of organisations with under 50 employees do so. The figure for partnerships is 37%, although another 20% of these plan to implement a formal programme.

New technology

- 80% of organisations had invested in new technology to improve customer care, ranging from fax machines to an integrated mainframe computer.

- Three quarters of respondents had automated processes in the last three years to give better service to customers, and a further 7% planned to do so.

- 86% of respondents whose organisations had invested in new technology felt that this had led to increased customer care.

- However, one in five respondents stated that there had been no investment in new technology over the last three years and none was planned.

Source: *Raising the Standard – A Survey of Managers' Attitudes to Customer Care*, Institute of Management

■ *How long do customer care programmes last?*

Should a programme run permanently once it's in place, or should you fix a time length for it? Managers were asked how long they expected their customer care programme to run; the survey did not discover the reason for the short expected duration of a few programmes.

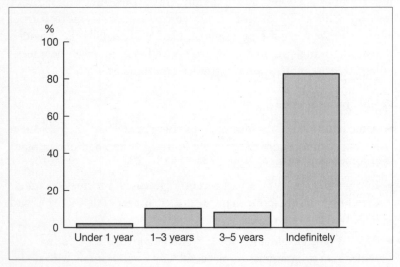

Source: *Raising the Standard – A Survey of Managers' Attitudes to Customer Care*, Institute of Management

Running a customer care programme

■ *What attitudes do managers have to customer care?*

What do you think is the main objective of customer care? Can a programme work without the full commitment of the chief executive or managing director? Can management impose quality standards on employees? There is some variation in managers' views of customer care, and it's worth making sure that you and your colleagues are all in agreement. You may find it useful to start by seeing whether you agree with the respondents in the Institute of Management survey, who were asked to state whether or not they agreed with a series of statements about customer care.

Statements	Strongly agree	Agree	Disagree	Strongly disagree	Don't know
The success of a customer care programme requires full commitment from the chief executive or managing director	82%	16%	1%	–	–
Everyone in an organisation has a customer	73%	25%	2%	–	1%
Management's role is to show by example a customer-caring, quality oriented attitude	65%	34%	1%	–	–
Customer care means defining and satisfying customers' needs and expectations	57%	41%	2%	–	1%

CUSTOMER CARE

Statements	Strongly agree	Agree	Disagree	Strongly disagree	Don't know
All employees should believe that their major concern is to ensure customer satisfaction	56%	38%	5%	–	1%
The main objective of customer care is to increase customer satisfaction and retain business	55%	41%	2%	–	1%
Quality standards cannot be imposed by management but must be accepted by all employees	51%	40%	7%	2%	–

Source: *Raising the Standard – A Survey of Managers' Attitudes to Customer Care,* Institute of Management

■ What do managers consider to be the main benefits of improving customer service?

Everybody goes on about how important and wonderful customer care programmes are, but what do you actually get out of them? Precisely what are these fabulous benefits? The Institute of Management asked respondents what the key benefits of improving customer care were for their organisations. The chief benefit seemed to be retaining existing customers. The following list shows what other important benefits were cited (each respondent was asked to identify three benefits).

Retention of existing customers	68%
Enhanced reputation of organisation	58%
Competitive advantage in the marketplace	53%
Attraction of new customers	43%
Increased profitability	28%
Improved staff morale and loyalty	25%
Cost efficiency	11%
Better productivity	10%
Other	2%

Source: *Raising the Standard – A Survey of Managers' Attitudes to Customer Care*, Institute of Management

■ *What do managers see as the main barriers to improving customer service?*

Customer care can't all be plain sailing – so what are the drawbacks? Well, you can't have a really effective programme unless everything is right. So the obvious question to ask is which things are most likely to go wrong? If you know in advance what the likely problems are, you have a better chance of avoiding them. The Institute of Management survey asked the same respondents to identify the three main barriers to improving customer care.

Emphasis on short term goals only	58%
Lack of commitment from top management	53%
Lack of training	47%
Lack of resources	34%
Lack of commitment from employees	32%
Lack of commitment from line management	31%
Cost constraints	24%
Effects of the recession	12%
Other	4%

Source: *Raising the Standard – A Survey of Managers' Attitudes to Customer Care*, Institute of Management

CUSTOMER CARE

■ *Should you train your staff in customer care?*

It's a bit silly to put all that investment into new technology and systems when you set up a customer care programme, if you're not going to invest in your employees as well. After all, they are the first line of customer care. But worryingly, few organisations seem to train their staff as thoroughly as they might. Only 6% of managers in this survey were very satisfied with the training they had been given – see the following chart. (The question they were asked concerned their satisfaction with staff training in general, not specifically their own training.)

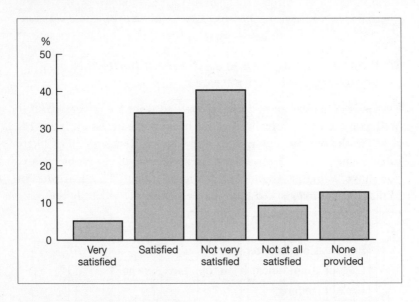

- One manager in eight in the survey had received no training whatsoever in customer service.

- When it comes to size, 14% of organisations with fewer than 50 employees have no customer service training; 8% with more than 5,000 employees also offer no training.

- Of those organisations without a formal programme, a quarter do not provide training in customer service either.

Source: Raising the Standard – A Survey of Managers' Attitudes to Customer Care, Institute of Management

CUSTOMER CONTACT

Keeping in touch

■ *Is it OK to initiate contact with your customers?*

You'll sell far more to your customers if you can keep in touch, let them know what new products and offers you have, and so on. But you don't want to offend them by invading their privacy. On the other hand, if you wait for *them* to approach *you*, you could wait for ever. So can you safely be the first to break the impasse? It rather depends on the type of contact. As a general rule, relevant, targeted communications will be welcomed by people who have bought from your company in the past. Customers are happy to receive some types of communication more readily than others, as the following chart shows.

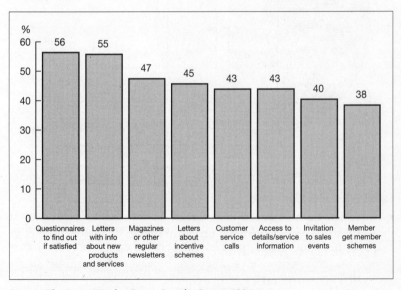

Source: *The Brann/Henley Centre Loyalty Survey 1994*

211

■ Can you predict how consumers will respond to direct communication with your company?

Of course, not every individual will behave in a totally predictable way. But the *Brann/Henley Centre Loyalty Survey* did find that the consumers they surveyed grouped into four distinct segments in terms of their attitudes to shopping, dialogue with companies, direct mail, the telephone and other related topics.

These segments give general guidelines that can help you find the best ways to communicate with existing and target customers. If you can identify which segment of the following chart your customers belong to, you can adjust your treatment of them accordingly.

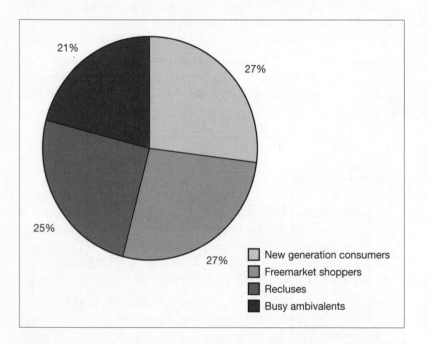

The two positive groups are both more likely to be female and to respond in a similar way to questions about the type of contact they would like from companies. They do, however, show subtle differences that are worth taking into account.

- *New generation consumers – 27%*. The people in this group tend to be younger. They are extremely positive about direct mail, are happy with using the telephone and are prepared to get involved in a dialogue with companies. Perhaps because they are younger, they do not feel they get too much direct mail (i.e. this may be a reflection of actual levels of receipt) but, importantly, they are sceptical about company motives despite being prepared to have a 'dialogue' with them.

- *Freemarket shoppers – 27%.* Apparently the beneficiaries of the Thatcher years, the people in this group – also more likely to be female – are very happy to involve themselves in a dialogue with companies which they generally appear to trust. They are extremely positive about the use of the telephone and, while they claim to get too much direct mail at present, they welcome most of the mailed communications suggested. This group's members are likely to be operating in the most markets – and appear to be confident, discerning shoppers.

The two negative segments are conversely more likely to be male, and generally reject most forms of direct communication and the concept of dialogue with companies. But here, too, there are subtle differences in attitude and motivation that are interesting.

- *The recluses – 25%.* Slightly more downmarket than any other group, and generally older, the people here appear to be operating outside the mainstream of consumer culture. Not only do they distrust companies; they also hate shopping and all forms of communication, particularly direct mail. They feel that they get too much direct mail even though common sense would suggest that they are unlikely to be a popular target audience. They participate in the fewest markets of all the segments, not surprisingly, and appear to offer little potential for any targeted marketing efforts.

- *The busy ambivalents – 21%.* A more recognisable group, and one that offers some potential if dealt with in the right way. These consumers are more likely to be working than those in the other groups and are slightly more upmarket. Like the *freemarket shoppers,* they operate in a number of markets, but are not keen on the idea of dialogue. Their attitudes towards mail and telephone are ambivalent rather than negative, suggesting that they may respond favourably in the right circumstances. However, they give the impression of being time-harried and too busy to entertain, let alone enjoy, direct communication.

Source: *The Brann/Henley Centre Loyalty Survey 1994*

CUSTOMER CARE

■ How do different consumer types respond to contact from companies?

The *freemarket shoppers* are over twice as likely as the *recluses* to welcome contact from companies. It seems that, if you can match your customers to these segments, you can learn a lot about their collective attitudes to communicating with your company.

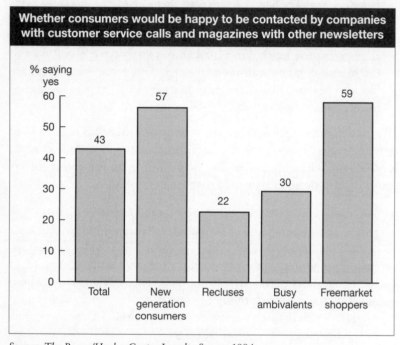

Whether consumers would be happy to be contacted by companies with customer service calls and magazines with other newsletters

Source: *The Brann/Henley Centre Loyalty Survey 1994*

■ What is the best way to keep in touch with customers at home?

There are a lot of options, of course. But what you need to know is which ones your customers prefer. The following chart shows what the customers in the survey considered to be the best methods.

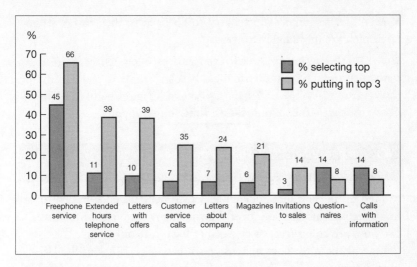

Source: *The Brann/Henley Centre Loyalty Survey 1994*

■ *How would consumers prefer to approach you for advice or information about a product?*

It's much easier to set up a customer care programme – which will enable your customers to contact you easily – if you know how they would prefer to contact you. In one survey, consumers were asked 'If you wanted advice or information about a product you had just purchased from a shop, how would you most like to go about getting this information?'

By taking the product back to the shop	51%
By telephoning the manufacturer's helpline	30%
By writing to the manufacturer	12%
Wouldn't do anything	5%
Don't know	2%

- Customers aged over 65 years old were most likely to go back to the shop (65%), while 35–44 year olds were most likely to call the manufacturer (38%).

- The general propensity was for the younger generations to be more inclined to phone and for the older generations to go back to the shop.

215

- Men are marginally more likely to go back to the shop or phone; women are more likely to write.

Source: *The Careline Report,* The L & R Group, 1995

Carelines

■ *What is a careline?*

A careline is a phone number dedicated to customer care. It is usually printed on the product packaging. Customers are encouraged to call for advice or information, or if they have any problems. Most calls to carelines are either free, or charged at local rate only.

One of the most comprehensive studies of carelines in the UK has been conducted by The L & R Group, a consultancy firm which helps clients to set up carelines. While they would clearly not want to present findings that undermined their own industry, this research is nonetheless conducted with thoroughness, and is highly regarded as being both valid and informative by many key people in the industry. We therefore considered it to be well worth including in this book.

■ *What kind of products or services are consumers most likely to use a careline for?*

Suppose you bought a packet of paper clips. It's unlikely that you would need to ring the manufacturer to ask how they worked, or to check that they weren't past their sell by date. But if you bought a vacuum cleaner, you might well want advice on how to fit the bag or whether it was safe to use on a wet floor. If you're wondering whether your organisation should set up a careline, you'll need to know whether your customers will want to call it. The following chart shows how likely the people surveyed thought they were to use a careline service for each of the product categories listed.

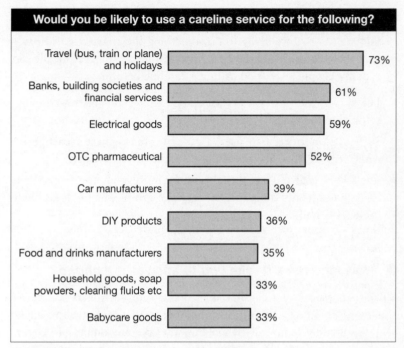

Would you be likely to use a careline service for the following?

Travel (bus, train or plane) and holidays	73%
Banks, building societies and financial services	61%
Electrical goods	59%
OTC pharmaceutical	52%
Car manufacturers	39%
DIY products	36%
Food and drinks manufacturers	35%
Household goods, soap powders, cleaning fluids etc	33%
Babycare goods	33%

Source: *The Careline Report*, The L & R Group, 1995

■ *Are consumers more likely to buy products that carry a careline number?*

One of the arguments that manufacturers give in favour of carelines is that they can increase the consumer's 'likelihood to buy', and their brand loyalty. So how true is this? Respondents were asked 'If you were buying a product and one of the choices was a brand which had a careline printed on the packaging, do you think you would be more likely to buy the brand with the helpline/careline?'

Yes – a lot more likely	17%
Yes – a little more likely	15%
No – makes no difference	67%
Don't know	2%

Source: *The Careline Report*, The L & R Group, 1995

■ *How many people have ever called a careline?*

People are often more likely to do something they have tried before –
getting them to do it for the first time can be the biggest hurdle. So
how many people have tried calling a careline before?

- The survey found that 26% of respondents had called a careline/
  helpline in the past.
- 38% of Londoners had used a careline (the highest area figure),
  while only 10% of Scots had done so (the lowest area figure).
- The 35–44 year old age group was the most likely to use carelines
  (35% had already done so); the 65+ age group was the least likely
  (only 14% had).

Source: *The Careline Report*, The L & R Group, 1995

■ *How long does it take you to answer the phone?*

Since the purpose of a careline is to make your customers feel better
looked after, it's clearly important to consolidate this feeling in the
way you handle their calls when they do take advantage of the service. The survey put UK carelines to the test, to see how long it took
them to answer the phone.

- The length of time varied between 1 and 20 seconds.
- The average length of time was 2.7 seconds.

Source: *The Careline Report*, The L & R Group, 1995

■ *Who answers your careline number?*

Your customer has dialled your number and it has been answered
efficiently. But who by? A machine or a real person? If you have yet
to decide what answering system to use, it might be worth knowing
how other companies answer their carelines.

In person	59%
Answer machine	14%
Voice activated or tone menu system	27%

Source: *The Careline Report*, The L & R Group, 1995

■ *Do you ask callers for their name and address?*

Can you wring the maximum benefit out of the call by asking your customers for their name and address so you can add it to your database – or is that pushing it too far? Presumably as people become more used to calling carelines, they will expect you to treat them in the same way that other careline operators do. So the question is, do the others use a careline call for data capture?

- 36% of callers to carelines in the UK are asked to give their name or address details.

Source: *The Careline Report*, The L & R Group, 1995

■ *Are consumers happy with the standard of carelines?*

The object of the exercise is to give the caller a warm glow and make them think what wonderful people you are. But is this what really happens? In the majority of cases, it seems that it is. But this isn't always the case. The following table shows how respondents who had used a careline in the past answered the question 'How happy were you with the service provided?'

Very unhappy	9%
Unhappy	4%
Neutral	15%
Happy	22%
Very happy	50%

- Women were less likely than men to be impressed: 17% of women were very unhappy compared to only 2% of men.
- The 65+ age group were most satisfied (73% were very happy); the least satisfied age group was 45–54 year olds, of whom 16% were very unhappy.

Source: The Careline Report, The L & R Group, 1995

■ *Do your competitors' products carry a careline number?*

It depends rather on what industry you're in; some have a higher careline penetration than others. This study measured penetration in terms of how many products out of ten in each category carried a careline number. The penetration is no more than 50% in any category, and the overall penetration level was 22%. However, this has grown from 8% two years earlier, and many people predict a huge growth in carelines (the overall penetration in the US is 80%, which shows what is possible).

Product	Products out of 10 which carry a careline number
Household products	2
Soft drinks	5
Babycare products	3
Paper products and female hygiene	1
Freezer cabinet	4
Chill cabinet	4
Dry goods	3
Canned foods	0
Over the counter (OTC) pharmaceuticals	0
Herbs, spices and cake ingredients	0

- Although the penetration of carelines has increased since the last study three years ago, this seems to be due less to an increase in the number of companies offering carelines, and more to companies extending the service across a brand portfolio.

Source: *The Careline Report*, The L & R Group, 1995

STANDARDS OF SERVICE

■ *Do you make specific commitments to your customers about customer care standards?*

You won't be very popular if you make claims you can't live up to. On the other hand, if you're confident that you can maintain the standards you set yourself, declaring them to your customers can only do you good. So how many companies feel confident enough to do this?

● More than 50% of organisations in one survey gave their customers specific guarantees about aspects of care such as delivery timescales, speed of answering the telephone and so on.

Source: *Raising the Standard – A Survey of Managers' Attitudes to Customer Care*, Institute of Management

■ *What's wrong with service in shops?*

It's very common to hear people complain about 'bad service' in shops, but what exactly do they mean? If you manage a retail outlet or a chain, you need to know what customers object to, in order to be sure of eliminating it from your shops. In this survey, consumers were asked which three or four things dissatisfied them most about the service they receive in shops nowadays. The list includes only the factors mentioned by 3% or more of the sample.

Unhelpful/uninterested staff	19%
Long queues at checkouts	19%
Rude/ignorant staff	11%
Poor customer service (slow)	9%
Unknowledgeable staff	8%
High prices/prices increasing	7%
Lack of sales assistants	6%
Poor choice of goods	5%
Staff standing around chatting	5%

CUSTOMER CARE

221

Pushy sales assistants	4%
Being pestered by sales staff/not left alone to browse	4%
Lack of personal service	4%
Not enough checkouts open	4%
Unfriendly, miserable staff	3%
Poorly trained staff	3%
Should have a separate till for cheque/credit card payers	3%
Lack of stock/goods out of stock	3%
Keep moving things around/difficult to find things	3%
Poor staff attitude (non-specific)	3%
Problems with staff – any	43%
None/nothing	19%
No answer	6%

Source: Consumer Concerns 1992, carried out by MORI for the National Consumer Council. Sample size: 1,978. The field work was carried out between 20 and 24 March 1992.

■ *How likely are customers to buy from you again after experiencing a problem with your customer service?*

The worst thing that is likely to happen as a result of poor customer service is that you lose customers. So how likely is it that your customers will desert you? It depends to some extent on the industry you're in. The following table shows whether customers in a range of industries intend to repurchase after an encounter that has been problematic, and after one that has been problem-free.

Industry	Percentage intending to repurchase	
	Problem	No problem
Financial services	56	81
Vehicle repair service	57	84
Telecommunications	83	95
Travel and leisure	82	97
Petrochemical products	80	94
Utility	75	78
Small package goods	72	96

Source: TARP

■ Why do customers switch their allegiance to one of your competitors?

When customers stop buying from you, it's tempting to assume that the reason is beyond your control; they have moved away, or no longer need that particular product or service. But is this really the case, or is the truth that you could have kept them coming back if you'd tried a little harder? One survey which asked customers why they changed suppliers found that in the majority of cases, better customer service could have prevented the defection. These are the reasons given:

The customer moved	3%
They developed a good relationship with another supplier	5%
They found a more competitive product elsewhere	9%
They were unhappy with the product	15%
They left because of no contact, indifference, or the attitude of the sales force	68%

Source: McGraw-Hill

COMPLAINTS

Customer attitudes and behaviour

■ Why do customers return goods to shops for an exchange or refund?

When people take goods back to the shop for an exchange or refund, is it because they inadvertently bought the wrong size or colour? Or are they returning an unwanted present? Occasionally, of course, it's because the goods are at fault in some way. Respondents were asked in one survey about an occasion in the last 12 months when they had returned goods to the shop where they bought them, and asked the reason why they sought an exchange or refund.

It wasn't the right size/didn't fit properly	32%
Damaged/faulty when bought	27%
Poor quality	10%
Developed fault/broke	8%
It wasn't right colour/style	6%
Unwanted present	6%
Dissatisfied with performance/didn't do what thought	5%
Food past sell by date/off	3%
Product unsafe	1%
Same product cheaper elsewhere	1%
Other	9%
Don't know	1%

Source: Consumer Concerns 1992, carried out by MORI for the National Consumer Council. Sample size: 1,978. The field work was carried out between 20 and 24 March 1992.

- So over half the people in the survey returned goods because they were below standard in some way. This suggests that you could substantially reduce returns in shops by improving the quality of the products.

■ How would customers prefer to approach you if they have a complaint about a product bought from a shop?

Before you start encouraging your customers to come forward with their complaints, you'll need to know how they want to approach you. It's no good laying on extra phone lines if they'd prefer to write, for example. So what do they want? The following table shows how respondents answered the question 'If you were not happy with the quality of goods and services you had just purchased, i.e. if you had just bought food which was contaminated or had a foreign body in it, which of the following would you most likely do?'

Go back to the shop from where you purchased the goods	67%
Write to the manufacturer to complain	16%
Ring the manufacturer's helpline to complain	11%
Never buy the product again	3%
Wouldn't do anything	1%
Don't know	1%

Source: *The Careline Report*, The L & R Group, 1995

■ How many of your customers do not contact you when confronted with a problem?

Some customers are straight on to the phone or marching up to the counter when they have a problem, and don't you just know it. But a surprising number of them never contact you at all. This is particularly disconcerting since it means you never even get to try and put things right. So how many complaints are left unarticulated? The following chart gives the percentages.

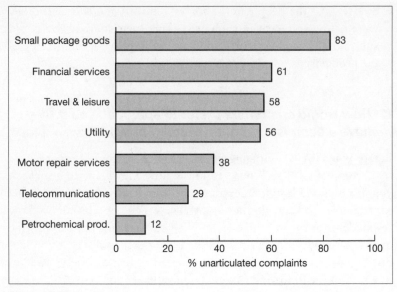

Source: TARP

■ *Do your customers keep their dissatisfaction to themselves because they are nervous of complaining?*

Although very few dissatisfied customers complain, lack of confidence doesn't seem to be one of the main reasons. The percentage of people who say they are confident about complaining (see the following chart) is substantially higher than the percentage of dissatisfied customers who – as we have just seen – actually do complain.

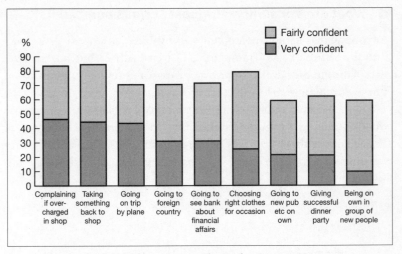

Source: *Planning for Social Change Survey*, The Henley Centre, 1994

■ *What do people hope to gain by complaining?*

When your customers make a valid complaint, what should you do about it? Give them a written apology? Or a refund? What are they actually after? Of course you could ask them – and it's a very good idea to do so – but if you're planning or reviewing your complaint handling system, it might help to know what most people generally want in recompense.

Improved service	39%
To get money/service eligible for	32%
To get an explanation	29%
Prevent same thing happening to others	28%
To get an apology	11%
To tell them what I thought of them	9%
To get compensation	7%
To vent anger/frustration	6%

Source: *MORI Research on Complaints Handling*, carried out for the Citizen's Charter Unit, 1997

■ *What are consumers' biggest serious complaints?*

Anyone with a serious complaint will probably, sooner or later, take it to the Office of Fair Trading, the Citizens' Advice Bureau, the relevant Trading Standards Department or some related organisation. These complaints are collected and analysed by the Office of Fair Trading, and give a good idea of the kind of problems people feel are worth pursuing with these authorities. In the first three months of 1995, almost three quarters of these complaints were about either sub-standard goods (47%), or selling techniques (26%) – see the following chart.

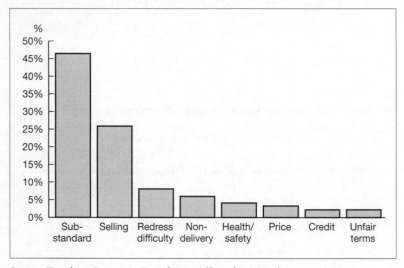

Source: *Trends in Consumer Complaints*, Office of Fair Trading

■ *How many people will your customers tell about their experience?*

The negative PR impact of unhappy customers telling their friends and colleagues what a dreadful organisation you are can be huge. The number of people they tell will depend on two key factors: was the problem they encountered large or small, and were they satisfied or dissatisfied with the way your organisation handled their complaint?

228

Size of problem	Median number of people told	
	Satisfied	Dissatisfied
Small problem	5	10
Large problem	8	16

Source: TARP

Handling the complaint

■ *Does it matter how quickly you respond to the complaint?*

Psychologists maintain that customers will be happy to wait longer for a solution to their problem if they are kept informed of what is going on, and reassured that something is being done. This suggests that you would do well to respond promptly to your customers' complaints, even if it takes a little longer to reach a final resolution. Certainly TARP's research seems to back this up. Precise results will vary between organisations, but here's an example of one company showing how complainants' satisfaction levels varied according to how speedily the company responded to them.

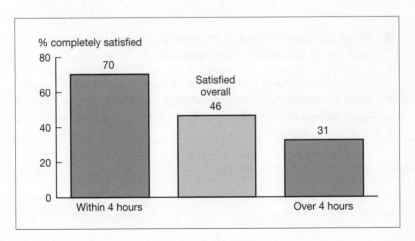

After this survey, the company in question set a new standard, so that all customers were contacted within four hours, if only for a status report.

Source: TARP 1995

■ Does it make a difference how many times the customer has to contact you to resolve the problem?

Have you ever had to contact a company or a supplier several times, just to get them to fix a problem? If so, you may not be surprised by the research findings here. Each time your dissatisfied customer has to contact you, the likelihood of their recommending your organisation to other people takes a nose-dive.

Number of contacts to resolve problem	Loyalty percentage (definitely/probably will recommend your organisation to others)
1	51
2	31
3 or more	16

Source: TARP

■ What do consumers think are the most important factors in handling a complaint?

There are a lot of things you can do to handle a complaint effectively, but it can be impractical – not to mention expensive – to do them all. So which factors do the general public think are the most important in handling a complaint?

Factor	Important factors	Single most important
Speed of response	52%	23%
Being kept informed	46%	17%
Fair investigation	40%	19%
Having a clear procedure	34%	10%
Friendliness and helpfulness	29%	6%
Named person dealing	25%	9%
Receiving written explanation	25%	5%
Receiving written apology	25%	5%
Investigation by senior staff	15%	5%
Receiving compensation	7%	2%

Source: *MORI Research on Complaints Handling*, carried out for the Citizen's Charter Unit, 1997

■ How much does it cost your organisation to deal with complaints?

Complaint handling can be expensive, although only 30% of organisations in one survey (all public service) actually knew how much complaints were costing them each year. What does seem clear is that the lower down the organisation a complaint is handled, the less expensive it is. The following table shows the costs stated by four of the public sector organisations in this survey, both for handling complaints informally through front line staff, and for passing them on for review by senior staff.

Organisation	Front line 'informal'	Review by senior staff
NHS Trust	£3–45	£370
Local Authority	£17	£110
Inland Revenue	£30–70	£78–650
Electricity company	£5–10	£80–140

- For these public service organisations, who have an Ombudsman, Adjudicator or Regulator to go to when complaints cannot otherwise be resolved, the costs of such an external review range between £150 and £11,200.

- The complaints systems and the basis for calculations in the figures above vary between organisations, and are therefore not directly comparable.

Source: *Putting Things Right*, The Citizen's Charter Complaints Task Force. Crown copyright is reproduced with the permission of the Controller of HMSO

■ *Who deals with letters of complaint?*

There are plenty of people who could take responsibility for answering letters of complaint, so who does it in your organisation? If you're thinking of formalising or changing your procedures on this point, it might help to know what other companies do. This was one of the questions covered in a survey of managers by the Institute of Management.

- Only 18% of letters were answered by customer services managers.

- About a third of letters were dealt with by the responsible employee's superior.

- A further third are dealt with by senior management or the managing director.

- The responsible employees themselves responded to 16% of letters of complaint.

Source: *Raising the Standard – A Survey of Managers' Attitudes to Customer Care*, Institute of Management

RELATIONSHIPS

Customers

■ *Does loyalty affect attitudes towards direct mail?*

Many companies – retailers particularly – think it does. Loyalty cards and bonus points illustrate how determined they are to maintain a quality customer relationship. The list of virtues that each company boasts grows – from looking after your children to mending your trolley; from cleaner petrol to responsible purchasing.

The Direct Mail Information Service researched the impact direct mailing had on loyalty. Judgements about direct mail begin with the outside of the envelope. So how much does relationship matter?

Likes	Dislikes
'I'm going to read that I'm a customer of theirs.'	'Your name has been specially selected from our computer – they think you're stupid.'
'If it's somebody I've had dealings with, then it's a good start – I know them and so I will see if it's something I'm interested in.'	

The relationship between a company and its customers was recognised by consumers in this survey as a reason in itself for mailing. A greater use of their personal data in the targeting and personalisation of a pack was then found acceptable.

Source: Consumer Creative Benchmarks, Direct Mail Information Service, 1995

CUSTOMER CARE

■ *Does personalising the message acknowledge the relationship?*

Mail is more likely to get attention if it is addressed to the recipient by name. But a personal appeal is not just personalisation of a letter. Recognition of any relationship is important. Generic titles such as Dear Donor or Dear Member met a mixed reception. Repeating the target's name in the main copy of the letter was seen as a cliché.

Likes	Dislikes
'I like mail to be personally addressed to me. It makes me feel that they've at least taken the time to do that.'	'It was "Dear Member". I thought, I've spent an arm or a leg on these, you could at least put "Dear Mrs X thank you for spending..."'
'The personal touch is rather nice. They've got my name there, you are not just a customer or an investor.'	'When your name is printed on each individual offer like that, it puts me off because I think they've just used your name on a printer, it's just standard. The personalised bit is out of it.'

Source: *Consumer Creative Benchmarks*, Direct Mail Information Service, 1995

Supply chain partnerships

■ *Are your supply chain relationships crucial to customer care?*

Most firms would answer yes. When Lloyds Banks and the Small Business Research Trust researched supply chain relationships, they found that an overwhelming 83% of respondents believe in having close relationships with suppliers. This was even though 79% agreed that 'there is plenty of choice of supplier'. Why does this happen? It is obviously easier to work with the known than the unknown but is this the only reason? No – there appears to be a two-way flow of information between companies and their suppliers.

- 61% agreed that 'my suppliers are an important source of information/advice to my business'.

- 32% thought it was the other way around – 'on balance, I provide help and guidance to my suppliers'.

Source: Quarterly Small Business Management Report, No. 1, Vol. 2, 1994, Lloyds Bank/Small Business Research Trust

■ *What do supply chain relationships require?*

Establishing and monitoring supply chain partnerships can be a tricky business. P-E International Logistics looked at the relationships which worked, and found they had certain requirements:

1 Information sharing
2 Regular meetings
3 Monitoring of the perceived benefits
4 Feedback to all concerned
5 The involvement of senior management.

Source: Supply Chain Partnerships – Who Wins? A survey into the opportunities and threats from supply chain partnerships. P-E International Logistics Consulting Services, in association with the Institute of Logistics, 1994

■ *Who drives outbound supply chains?*

Nearly all companies believe that it is their customers rather than themselves who drive outbound supply chains:

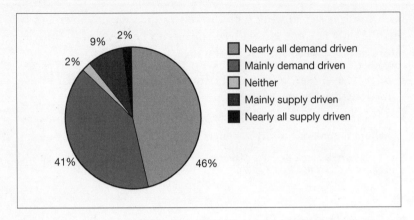

The movement towards customer domination will, if anything, intensify in the future:

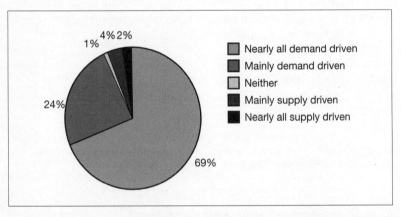

Source: Supply Chain Partnerships – Who Wins? A survey into the opportunities and threats from supply chain partnerships. P-E International Logistics Consulting Services, in association with the Institute of Logistics, 1994

■ *Who drives inbound supply chains?*

If customers drive outbound supply chains, how much affect do they have on inward supply chains? Most companies believe that they drive their relationships with their suppliers.

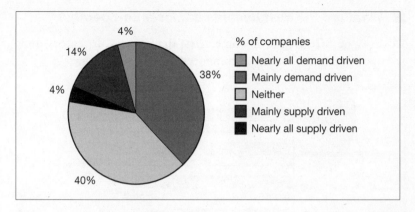

Source: Supply Chain Partnerships – Who Wins? A survey into the opportunities and threats from supply chain partnerships. P-E International Logistics Consulting Services, in association with the Institute of Logistics, 1994

■ *How willing are companies to discuss logistics costs openly with their partners?*

If costs can be cut, then the customer will always benefit. So how open are companies about costs? Only 1 in 4 companies discuss their costs with their suppliers; only 1 in 8 discuss their costs with their customers:

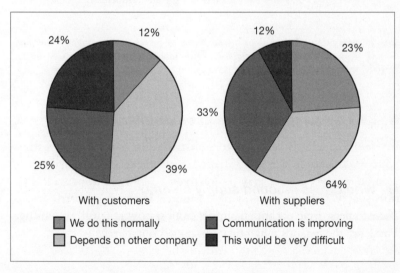

Source: Supply Chain Partnerships – Who Wins? A survey into the opportunities and threats from supply chain partnerships. P-E International Logistics Consulting Services, in association with the Institute of Logistics, 1994

■ *What are the cost benefits of closer co-operation?*

Cost savings are greater in some areas than others. Inventory and transport were seen as the most important areas for cost saving:

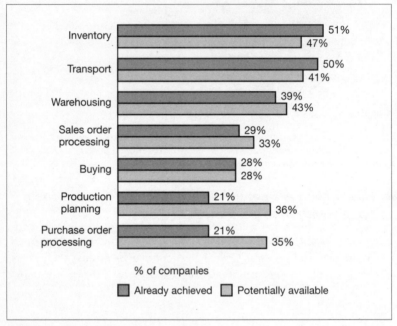

Source: *Supply Chain Partnerships – Who Wins? A survey into the opportunities and threats from supply chain partnerships.* P-E International Logistics Consulting Services, in association with the Institute of Logistics, 1994

■ *Why do companies outsource distribution?*

If you are currently meeting your distribution requirements within your organisation, are you satisfied with the service that you provide? If you are not, it may interest you to know that providers of third-party services are playing an increasing part in distribution. Their market share of the total distribution market is still increasing. These are the reasons why other companies outsource:

Reason	Companies who cited reason
Increase flexibility	69%
Improve service	57%
Reduce cost	55%
Avoid investment	45%
Non-core activity	40%
Obtain specialist management	33%
Improve control	30%

Source: *Contracting Out or Selling Out? Survey into the current issues concerning outsourcing distribution.* P-E International Logistics Consulting Services, in association with the Institute of Logistics, 1993

■ What are the main problems about outsourcing?

You may well be satisfied with your contractors overall, but experiencing some problems. Or perhaps you are considering outsourcing, but feel that forewarned is forearmed. So what are the problems likely to be? Companies were asked to identify the main problem areas:

Problem area	Proportion of companies experiencing the problem
Insufficient management information	27%
Management issues	23%
Level of cost	20%
Service failures	17%
Lack of flexibility	13%

Source: *Contracting Out or Selling Out? Survey into the current issues concerning outsourcing distribution.* P-E International Logistics Consulting Services, in association with the Institute of Logistics, 1993

■ What are the causes of these problems?

If things aren't running smoothly, you will probably be responsible, at least in part. Companies are honest enough to admit their share of the blame:

CUSTOMER CARE

Cause of problem area	Proportion of companies citing cause
Insufficient controls	36%
Poor contractor management	32%
Inadequately specified contracts	20%
Insufficient information supplied	20%
Failure of client management	18%

Source: Contracting Out or Selling Out? Survey into the current issues concerning outsourcing distribution. P-E International Logistics Consulting Services, in association with the Institute of Logistics, 1993

GIVING THE
RIGHT IMPRESSION

MEDIA RELATIONS

Image

If you're easily frightened, it's quite terrifying how much impact a seemingly tiny factor can have on the way your customers view you. This view, in turn, can affect their loyalty to you and even whether they remain customers at all. Of course, once you understand how your behaviour affects your customers' attitudes there are huge benefits; you can influence your customers in the way you choose.

■ How important is media image?

Brand image is a key concern for advertisers. Media image – how consumers' perceptions of the advertising medium reflect back on the messages they receive – is less often considered. This applies across all media – from direct mail to radio and TV advertising.

■ How important is it to get the creative right first time?

Creative work has to reflect what consumers think is appropriate to that sector. A Direct Mail Information Service survey found that a mailing from a charity offering a prize draw was widely condemned as a waste of resources. The most important requirement appeared to be that professional companies look professional.

Likes	Dislikes
'It looks professional – it's coming from a professional company. It's got their logo on it, it's got the window with the letter inside ... it's the right way of doing it.'	'If that was the first thing I'd ever received from them, I wouldn't be terribly impressed ... terribly unprofessional, and yet they are a big concern.'

Source: Consumer Creative Benchmarks, Direct Mail Information Service, 1995

■ *Will creative be affected by which sector you're in?*

One of the most complex dimensions of this perception is product sector. Consumers may have strong views about which form of advertising is acceptable from which product sector and resist a break from traditional advertising methods for that sector. Some categories of goods have a built-in relevance which makes them acceptable even if mistargeted. Few people mind receiving information about cars which are above their income bracket. Yet information about loans sent to a low income household might be considered intrusive.

Likes	Dislikes
'If it's something that I am interested in, then I assume that they've taken time out, they know something about me, I've bought something at another place and they've matched me up with this product.'	'They don't need to do that. I love condensed books and I subscribe to the monthly magazine and I'm getting that rubbish all the time. Now I just think, "Oh God, not more".'
'There are companies I wouldn't mind hearing from.'	'Where did they get my name?'

Source: *Consumer Creative Benchmarks*, Direct Mail Information Service, 1995

■ *How will it affect your image if you write to your customers to keep them in touch with your organisation?*

Even something as simple as writing – or failing to write – to your customers can make a big difference to how favourably they view your organisation. In one piece of research, consumers were asked how they would view a company if it sent them certain types of letters or mailshots. The results are shown in the following chart.

GIVING THE RIGHT IMPRESSION

243

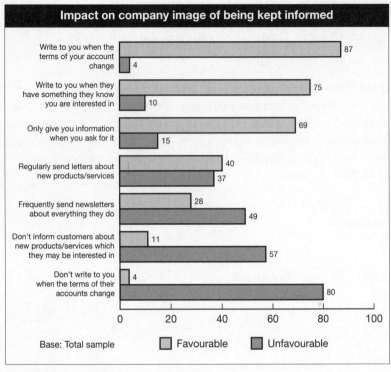

Impact on company image of being kept informed

Statement	Favourable	Unfavourable
Write to you when the terms of your account change	87	4
Write to you when they have something they know you are interested in	75	10
Only give you information when you ask for it	69	15
Regularly send letters about new products/services	40	37
Frequently send newsletters about everything they do	28	49
Don't inform customers about new products/services which they may be interested in	11	57
Don't write to you when the terms of their accounts change	4	80

Base: Total sample

Source: Direct Mail Information Service

■ *What effect are you having on business people if you send them inaccurate or duplicated mailshots?*

An average of one in three business mailings contains some form of error in the address. Not only does this often prevent your mailshot from ever reaching its target, but it also creates an inefficient and uninterested image of your company.

- 78% of business people think that an inaccurate address reflects badly on the organisation that sent the mailshot.
- 72% of business people agree that duplicate mail 'annoys them intensely'.

Source: Direct Mail Information Service

Branding

■ *How consistent are consumers in the types of products they buy?*

There is a tendency to pigeonhole consumers, and to assume that they will be consistent in the types of product that they buy, and loyal to certain brands. But is this really true, or are most people more capricious in their shopping patterns than we imagine? It's very difficult to plan for a new product, for example, unless you have an idea of how popular it's going to be. Research suggests that you can't rely too heavily on how consumers respond to one product when predicting how they will respond to another. Here's an example from one study:

● Use of an environmentally friendly brand in one category does not necessarily translate into other categories. People make token brand purchases to assuage their consciences. A similar pattern occurs in relation to foods that are supposed to be 'better for you'. Simply because someone buys low fat yoghurt and low fat dairy spread, does not mean they will buy reduced fat biscuits or low fat mayonnaise.

Source: The Research Business Group, 1995

■ *Are people more likely to notice a new brand in some product areas than others?*

If you're launching a new brand and want to persuade consumers to buy it, the first thing you need to do is to get them to notice it on the shelves. Researchers have accompanied people shopping to study how they choose items, and have made some useful discoveries.

● There are low, medium and high interest areas within a supermarket and, in general, the lower the interest, the more automatic the purchase decision. So it is more difficult for a new brand or brand variant (e.g. jam) to be noticed among items classified by consumers as commodities or essentials (such as tea, butter, tinned fruit and vegetables, cheese and so on), than it is in the areas of chilled products, deli foods, fruit and veg, bakery products and personal toiletries.

Source: The Research Business Group, 1995

GIVING THE RIGHT IMPRESSION

■ *How do consumers perceive own label products?*

We often assume that people buy own label products simply because of the price, but research indicates that there are many other possible reasons. If you are competing against own label products, price is not the only thing they have on their side. Here's one example:

● Women who are dieting at the time of purchase often buy the own label variant of a product in order to reinforce their deprivational mind-set. Advertised brands are seen to be too rewarding in terms of visual cues and product quality.

Source: The Research Business Group, 1995

Sponsorship

■ *What does it cost to make sponsorship pay?*

The answer to this question seems to be received wisdom in the PR industry, and although the research appears to be anecdotal rather than scholarly, it is useful enough to be well worth including here. If you sponsor anything from the local school choir to a national football team, you are doing it – at least in part – because you want the publicity. But you will have to pay extra for the publicity. (To give you a simple example, if you want your football team to wear your name on their shirts, you'll have to provide the shirts.)

● The amount you have to spend in PR, advertising and so on, to make your sponsorship effective will be at least as much again as the value of the original sponsorship.

Source: The Research Business Group, 1995

Editorial coverage

■ *How much more likely to be seen and read is your editorial than your advertisements?*

People will tell you that if you can get press releases placed, they are more likely to be read. But how much more likely? It depends to some extent on the type of publication, but the figures are pretty similar. The following charts are indexed to 100, where 100 is the seeing (or reading) level for advertising.

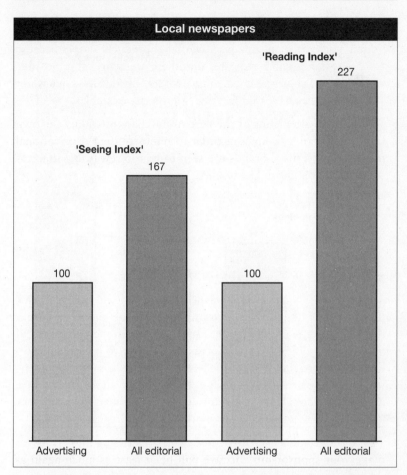

Source: Welbeck Golin/Harris Communications Limited and The National Dairy Council

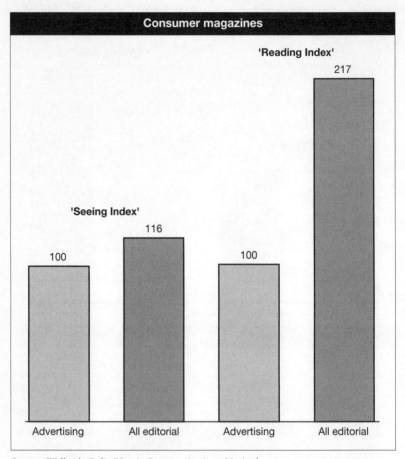

Consumer magazines

'Reading Index'
217

'Seeing Index'
116

100

100

| Advertising | All editorial | Advertising | All editorial |

Source: Welbeck Golin/Harris Communications Limited

■ *How can you make sure that your editorial hits the mark?*

Colin Wheildon, an experienced Australian writer and journalist, tells the following cautionary tale:

> There was a government decision to turn street lights off at 9 p.m. to save energy. Police claimed the move would lead to increased crime. The article's headline was 'Let there be light, police chief pleads'. Comprehension of the article was about 5%, as 50% of readers don't go past the headline. A dummy page was produced with the identical article, and the headline 'Blackout will help criminals, police claim.' The comprehension level soared to 64%. So keep it simple.

He has five top tips for writing effective editorial:

- Place yourself in the position of your reader or customer
- Try to read your publication as though you were interested in responding to the message
- Make sure everything is kept simple
- Don't be too clever
- Don't let the design get in the way of the message.

Source: Colin Wheildon 1997

■ *Which of the various types of editorial are most likely to be read?*

There are plenty of different kinds of editorial techniques you can use. Which are the most likely to attract attention? Once again, it depends on the publication, but the results are not that different.

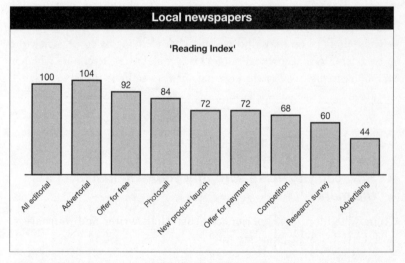

Source: Welbeck Golin/Harris Communications Limited and The National Dairy Council

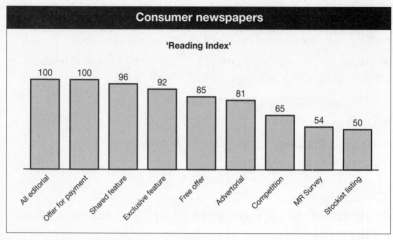

Source: Welbeck Golin/Harris Communications Limited

■ *Which types of editorial in local newspapers get most read?*

If you want to maximise the chances of your editorial being read, it helps to know which pages the readers are most likely to look at (see the following chart). You may find it somewhat challenging to present your press release as a horoscope, but you may well be able to choose whether to emphasise the local or the national angle, or write to the letters page.

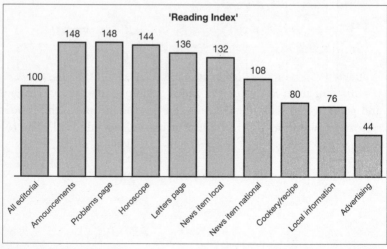

Source: Welbeck Golin/Harris Communications Limited and The National Dairy Council

■ How much does editorial reading in local papers vary by different subjects?

Are you writing on a subject that the readers want to know about? Here's a guide to the most popular subjects in local papers.

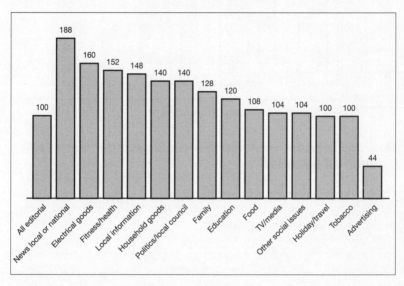

Source: Welbeck Golin/Harris Communications Limited and The National Dairy Council

■ Does branded, PR-led editorial get less read than magazine originated editorial?

Branded editorial makes branded or generic promotional references. It's different from 'advertorial', which is simply advertising designed and presented to look like editorial. So do readers approach branded editorial any differently from the magazine's own editorial? The following chart shows that it is marginally less likely to be read.

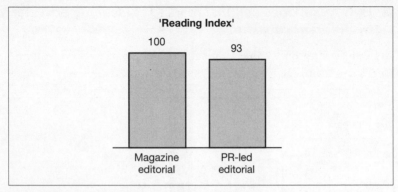

'Reading Index'

Source: Welbeck Golin/Harris Communications Limited

■ Does branded editorial in local papers get less read than all editorial?

Does the same rule follow for local papers as for consumer magazines? In fact, your branded editorial is slightly less likely to be read, as shown by the following chart.

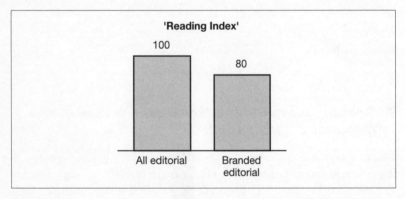

'Reading Index'

Source: Welbeck Golin/Harris Communications Limited and The National Dairy Council

■ Does a magazine add believability to branded editorial? And does it vary between magazines?

If you include branded editorial in a consumer magazine, does some of the magazine's authority rub off on you? See the following gauge.

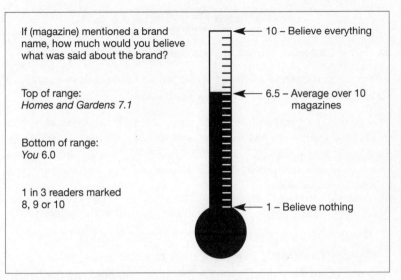

If (magazine) mentioned a brand name, how much would you believe what was said about the brand?

10 – Believe everything

Top of range:
Homes and Gardens 7.1

6.5 – Average over 10 magazines

Bottom of range:
You 6.0

1 in 3 readers marked 8, 9 or 10

1 – Believe nothing

Source: Welbeck Golin/Harris Communications Limited

■ *Does a newspaper add believability to branded editorial? Does it vary between papers?*

And what about local papers? The level of believability is not quite so high as it is for consumer magazines.

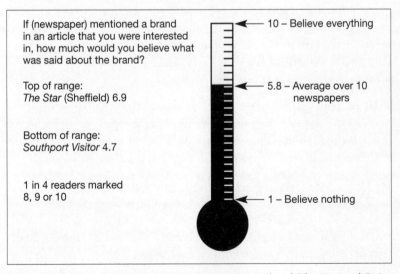

If (newspaper) mentioned a brand in an article that you were interested in, how much would you believe what was said about the brand?

10 – Believe everything

Top of range:
The Star (Sheffield) 6.9

5.8 – Average over 10 newspapers

Bottom of range:
Southport Visitor 4.7

1 in 4 readers marked 8, 9 or 10

1 – Believe nothing

Source: Welbeck Golin/Harris Communications Limited and The National Dairy Council

Press Relations

■ *How can you improve your handling of the media?*

The Aziz Corporation advises a wide range of companies on effective techniques for handling the media. Khalid Aziz, its founder, warns:

> *A poor performance in front of the media can have an adverse impact on both the individual's and the company's standing. During a crisis, when facing a hostile press, any uncertainty or a failure to field difficult questions can lead to a public relations disaster and have a severe impact on reputation and share price.*

Khalid Aziz has four main tips for those charged with talking to the press:

1 Do your homework. Before agreeing to an interview, take time to find out what the publication or programme is about, its readership or audience, and the angle the journalist is looking for. This will enable you to give answers tailored to the journalist's target audience, making you a useful contact for the future and will ensure you do not get caught out.

2 Exploit your opportunity. While your initial reaction may be reluctance to talk to the press for fear of misrepresentation, with careful preparation and training it is possible to use the opportunity to score points for your organisation. If you can also provide interesting and informative comment when called upon, journalists will grow to value your contribution to a story, enabling you to improve the media profile of your company.

3 Be on your guard. Never be lulled into a false sense of security, no matter how friendly the journalist. Speaking 'off the record' is a trap many people fall into. Journalists have a job to do and, regardless of whether a comment is on or off the record, headline-making news is headline-making news. Do not say anything that you would not be prepared to see published or broadcast.

4 Rehearse. When taking part in an interview for television or radio, you will be placed in unfamiliar surroundings and in front of high-tech lighting, camera and recording equipment. This can be unsettling and, as some people do freeze in front of the camera, it is a good idea to rehearse with colleagues beforehand. Anticipate difficult questions and how you would answer them. Many people go to professional organisations specialising in media handling in order to practise in front of a camera in a non-threatening environment. This allows you to check how you come across on camera and to receive expert advice on how to give a truly professional, confident performance.

Source: Khalid Aziz, The Aziz Corporation

Crisis management

■ *What are the most common mistakes in crisis planning?*

Few companies prepare properly for a PR crisis. It could be an accident at the factory, a round of redundancies, local unpopularity over pollution or planning permission, or perhaps a dangerously faulty product that you sold to someone who has taken their complaint to the media. Whatever the cause, a PR crisis can inflict huge damage on your organisation and its profits if you are unprepared.

Regester Larkin is a PR consultancy that specialises in crisis management. After years of experience, they have built up a picture of where people usually go wrong, and what steps they could take to avoid turning a drama into a crisis. They have found that the most common mistakes at the planning stage are:

- Assuming a crisis will only happen to someone else.

- Believing that crises cannot be anticipated and planned for.

Source: Regester Larkin Ltd

■ *What are the key steps for successful crisis planning?*

So what can you do to avert disaster by being prepared before it strikes?

The 5 key steps to avert disaster
1 Identify areas of risk in the business 2 Identify audience groups that will need to be communicated with 3 Develop crisis communication procedures 4 Train spokespeople and telephone response support teams 5 Test procedures and training programmes through annual exercise simulations

Source: Regester Larkin Ltd

■ *What are the most common mistakes in crisis handling?*

Once the storm strikes, the advance preparation all seems worthwhile. But there are still right and wrong ways to cope with the crisis. Again, Regester Larkin's experience is that the commonest mistakes people and organisations make when handling a PR crisis are:

Ignoring the media until the crisis has been resolved operationally.

Speculating about the cause of the crisis.

Fielding an inarticulate spokesperson to communicate about the crisis.

Fielding several spokespeople who communicate conflicting messages.

Underestimating the level of public/media concern about the crisis.

Adopting a combative stance with the media during the crisis.

Relying solely on lawyers for advice on how to resolve the crisis.

Ignoring independent, authoritative 'friends' who could support the organisation's cause during the crisis.

Source: Regester Larkin Ltd

■ *What are the key steps for successful crisis handling?*

That's a fairly thorough list of what you shouldn't do during a crisis. So what have the experts found to be the most important things that you *should* do?

The 5 key steps for successful crisis handling

1 Take full account of likely public perceptions of the decisions you take
2 Explain what has happened, what steps are being taken to remedy the problem, and that the organisation cares about what has happened
3 Talk about people first, environment second, property third and financial consequences fourth
4 Identify 'friends' to speak out on the organisation's behalf
5 Keep employees informed of developments on a regular basis

Source: Regester Larkin Ltd

PUBLIC RELATIONS

Measuring the effectiveness of PR

■ *How can you assess the value of your PR?*

It's all very well dashing off press releases and splashing out on sponsorship, but how can you tell if it's working? What you need is some way to measure how effective it is, so you know whether your PR activities are an investment or a drain. What's more, since you probably use several different types of PR, you want to know how each one is working.

Since PR evaluation is such a complex topic, it is impossible to come up with truly quantitative and useful data. But qualitative research has been conducted. Dr Tom Watson of Hallmark Marketing Services recently carried out the first major study of public relations evaluation in the UK, so it seems helpful to include a summary of his findings here. To evaluate PR effectively, he says you must be clear on the objectives of the activity.

Media-based programmes

If your PR activity is mostly carried out in the media, here's how you can evaluate the results.

- Check that the programme's messages are being received and interpreted correctly by checking the content of media coverage.

- Review which journalists and publications are positive, neutral or negative about your product, service or organisation.

- Track issues which are relevant to your business or organisation.

Media analysis can be undertaken in-house, but look out for 'observer bias' when interpreting results. There are several media analysis firms in the UK which use independent reader panels and sophisticated software.

- Beware the substitution game. Media analysis mainly measures the effectiveness of PR *output*. It usually doesn't tell of the impact of the message. For judgements on impact, study the attitudes of your target audience through quantitative (surveys, sales responses, enquiries) or qualitative (focus groups, panels, audits) methods.

- Be wary also of valuations of media analysis data which assess the quantity but not the quality of coverage, such as Advertising Value Equivalent (also known as Advertising Cost Equivalent). These give a monetary value to the editorial coverage in terms of advertising space costs, but they have no statistical validity and attempt to give a value to something which would not have been purchased anyway.

Multi-strategy programmes

Not all PR programmes are carried out only in the media. Many business-to-business campaigns use contact programmes, seminars and events, and corporate entertainment. Lobbying, community relations and publications may be the main strategies for others. The key evaluation points are:

- Use research to help set objectives.
- Select the key messages you want to put forward.
- Use surveys, audits, media analysis and informal feedback to judge effectiveness.
- Create an information loop to change and vary the campaign: if you run a continuous PR programme you can constantly feed back information from evaluation and monitoring into the continued development of the programme.

Avoid information clutter. By choosing separate messages for different promotional methods, such as advertising that pushes a price message and PR pulling through the case for expertise or product/service benefits, the relative effectiveness of each method can be tracked.

Source: Hallmark Marketing Services

Using an agency

■ *On what basis do you pay your PR agency?*

You don't have to pay a straight fee; and many companies don't. One survey of large companies from a cross-section of industries showed that although the most common method of payment is by a straight fee, others are occasionally used as well. (A few companies use more than one method of payment, which is why the percentages add up to more than 100.) The main methods are:

Payment for results	3%
Commission/percentage	4%
Straight fees	70%
Payment for ideas	3%
Other	5%
Not stated	45%

Source: Richmond Events Limited

■ *How often should you review your relationship with your PR agency?*

A regular review session with your agency is important to make sure that you're still getting the best out of the relationship, and to identify and iron out any problems or tensions. But what's the norm?

Annually	25%
Every six months	9%
Every quarter	3%
Continually – project by project	8%
No fixed period of time	30%
Not applicable	13%
Not stated	12%

Source: Richmond Events Limited

Internal PR

■ *How are employees told about what goes on at their place of work, and are they able to give feedback?*

Internal PR is crucial. If your staff are not happy, their morale drops, staff turnover increases, productivity goes down, and your reputation in the community is seriously damaged. And communication is central to good PR. There are various ways of letting your employees know what is happening in your organisation, some of which provide more opportunity for feedback than others. If you are using only noticeboards and newsletters to spread news, are you giving your employees a fair chance to have their say? And if not, will their opinion of you as an employer be diminished?

- 75% of employees in this survey reported that they received information through notices or news sheets.

- Information meetings were held to keep 70% of employees up to date.

- 63% of people surveyed were in organisations which held meetings in which they could express their views.

Source: *Employee Commitment And The Skills Revolution*, Policy Studies Institute, 1993

■ Are employees satisfied with the level of communication they receive?

On the face of it, the present level of internal communication in British companies seems acceptable. But if you are in line with current practice, is this good enough, or is it likely that your employees' morale could be improved still further?

- Overall, 30% of employees said they were 'completely' or 'very' satisfied with the level of internal communication in their company.

- Another 42% were 'fairly' satisfied with the communication level.

- Only 29% of those surveyed were ambivalent or dissatisfied with internal communications.

- The level of dissatisfaction was generally much higher in larger companies: 46% of those in companies with less than 10 employees were 'completely' or 'very' satisfied, as against 19% in companies with 100–499 employees and 21% in those with over 500 employees.

Source: *Employee Commitment And The Skills Revolution*, Policy Studies Institute, 1993

■ What forms of internal communication increase employee satisfaction with communication levels?

If you want to change the level of communication within your organisation, you will want to know what measures have the greatest effect on increasing employee satisfaction.

- The provision of written information does not seem to have a great effect on satisfaction levels.

- Employees who are involved in information-giving meetings are generally more satisfied, with 4% more saying that they are 'completely' or 'very' satisfied and 20% fewer being dissatisfied to any degree.

- Setting up meetings where employees can air their views seems by far the most effective method, with 12% more of these employees being 'completely' or 'very' satisfied, and the proportion of dissatisfied staff plummeting from 44% to 20%.

Source: *Employee Commitment And The Skills Revolution*, Policy Studies Institute, 1993

■ *What is the most effective channel for communication?*

If you make decisions about the internal communication procedures in your company, then it is up to you to minimise misunderstandings and failed communication. So if you really want to get the message across clearly, and make sure it is understood, what is the best way to communicate it? Not in writing, it seems.

- Over 67% of managers said that they found face-to-face communication to be more effective than any method based on paper or technology.
- Under 50% of managers said that they found paper-based communication to be effective.

Source: *Are Managers Getting The Message?* Institute of Management, 1992

■ *How many companies have internal magazines or newsletters?*

One obvious way to improve internal PR, and to instill a feeling of community among employees, is to have a magazine or newsletter that deals with internal company issues and news. If you don't make use of this approach to internal communication, are you overlooking a valuable and widely used resource, or are you treating it with the usual level of scepticism? The following table shows what proportion of organisations have newsletters or magazines, broken down by size (more or less than 300 employees) and ownership (British or foreign).

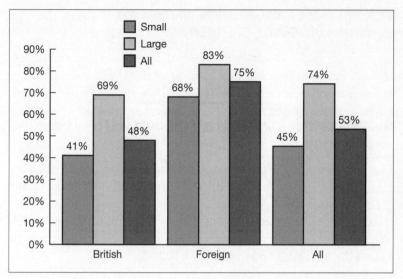

Source: *Consultation And Communication*, ACAS, 1990

■ *Are internal communications improving?*

Internal PR can be a major issue in many companies, but how often do revisions of the procedures actually take place, and how effective are these changes? One survey asked managers if their internal communication systems had changed over the last two years.

- 60% of them said yes, it had.
- Unfortunately, only 40% of these said that their internal communications strategy was now clearer than it had been.

Source: *Are Managers Getting The Message?* Institute of Management, 1992

GIVING THE
RIGHT IMPRESSION

SALES PROMOTIONS

Christmas gifts

■ *What sort of Christmas gifts should you give your customers?*

The best gifts are the ones that will be seen frequently by the customer, over a long period, and are considered acceptable (alcohol, for example, is not always suitable). Not surprisingly, the ubiquitous calendar is the most popular choice. The following table shows which gifts are most often sent (some companies send more than one type of gift, so the total adds up to more than 100%).

Type of gift	Percentage of companies sending
Business calendar	94
Alcohol	15
Key fobs	8
Clocks/calculators/ties	9

Source: Bemrose 1992

■ *How much do you spend on Christmas gifts?*

Small businesses are, traditionally, the greatest senders of Christmas gifts, because a well planned gift is a highly cost effective form of promotion.

• In 1992, the average small business spent between £2,000 and £10,000 on gifts.

Source: Bemrose 1992

Competitions

■ How much do you spend on prizes, and how many do you give?

You could hand out a top-of-the-range car to the first 100 prizewinners, or you could just give a Crackerjack pencil to the top three entrants. The kind of prizes you give can say a lot about whether your organisation is generous or mean-spirited. Of course, it has a lot to do with what the other organisations in your industry are doing; consumers expect a better prize from a washing machine manufacturer than they do from a charity. The matrix that follows shows the typical number of prizes, and their value, for several industry types.

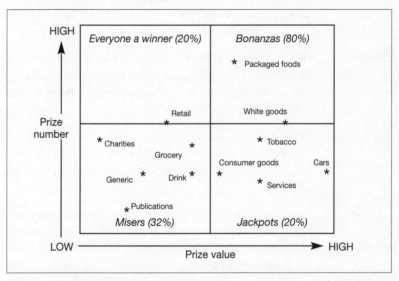

Source: *Sales Promotion Competitions – A Survey*, Sue Peattie and Ken Peattie, Journal of Marketing Management, 1993

■ How can you make sure your competition is a success?

After studying over two and a half thousand competitions, the authors of one survey had developed a pretty good idea of the key factors for success. Planning seems to be everything, and they put together a list of guidelines for planning competitions which they entitled mnemonically the COMPETE checklist.

Co-sponsors Will the competition be run by the company or shared with another retailer or manufacturer? If so, how will costs and responsibilities be divided?

Objectives What are the marketing objectives of the competition? What message will it send to consumers and what effect should it produce? Is it only short term sales uplifts, or are there more long term objectives such as generating new users or raising product awareness?

Mechanics How will the competition be designed, delivered, entered and judged? How can the mechanics of the competition best support its objectives? What could go wrong logistically and how could it be prevented?

Prizes What number and value of prizes will be needed to make the competition attractive? Can the prizes be chosen to reinforce the product concept? What prizes will attract target consumers?

Expenditure How much of the marketing budget and the time of marketing management should the competition consume? How can the judging be made as simple as possible?

Timing Should the competition be used to counteract seasonal lows, reinforce seasonal highs or 'spoil' rivals' promotions? Should the gap between launch and closing date be long to maximise the effect, or short to prevent loss of consumer interest? How long should special packs, leaflets and so on be available for?

Evaluation How will the effectiveness of the competition be measured in terms of achieving its objectives? Who should be responsible for evaluation, when, and using what measures?

Source: Sales Promotion Competitions – A Survey, Sue Peattie and Ken Peattie, *Journal of Marketing Management*, 1993

Using an agency

■ On what basis do you pay your sales promotion agency?

As with PR, you don't have to pay a straight fee. The list below shows the results of a survey of large companies from a cross-section of industries. (A few companies use more than one method of payment, which is why the percentages add up to more than 100.)

Payment for results	3%
Commission/percentage	6%
Straight fees	43%
Payment for ideas	5%
Other	5%
Not stated	40%

Source: Richmond Events Limited

■ How often should you review your relationship with your sales promotion agency?

If you don't review your relationship regularly, you risk missing opportunities to improve it further, and there's a chance it could deteriorate badly. So it's wise to set review dates, but how frequent do they need to be? Here's what the organisations in this survey do:

Annually	8%
Every six months	6%
Every quarter	3%
Continually – project by project	18%
No fixed period of time	21%
Not applicable	19%
Not stated	25%

Source: Richmond Events Limited

DESIGN, PRINT AND THE WRITTEN WORD

Much of the information in this section has been taken from a study of the validity – or invalidity – of certain elements of typographic design. This study, called *Communicating or just making pretty shapes*, is a treasure store of information for anyone who is doing their own typesetting and design, and for people who find themselves briefing designers. The information in this section represents only part of the full report.

To help you understand the following results, it is worth explaining briefly how Colin Wheildon, the author of the study, measured people's comprehension for the purposes of these tests. The respondents were given several pages, each of which contained a single article. They read the articles, under supervision, and in a given time, were then asked a series of questions. They were not told that the questions would attempt to determine the level of comprehension.

Answers were rated: ten to seven correct, good; six to four, fair; three to none, poor. The respondents were divided into two equal groups to provide a measure of control. The tests were repeated in various forms throughout a seven-year period.

In addition to this, the respondents were asked a number of qualitative questions during the course of the research programme to establish any other effects of the elements of typography.

Layout

■ *How can you design the layout of a page to encourage people to read it?*

Whether you're designing an ad or a sales brochure, the way you lay out the page can have a marked effect on whether your targets choose to read it or not.

According to the research:

On any page where there is writing or printing, the starting point is the upper left corner. Here the eye, trained from babyhood, enters a page, and here it must be caught by an attention compeller. When the eye reaches the lower right corner, after scanning across and down progressively, the reading task is finished. Reading gravity doesn't follow a straight line; it moves to right and left, and has to be lured to what are called the fallow corners by optical magnets, usually illustrations. The eye does not willingly go against reading gravity, with the obvious exception that, having read a line of type or writing, it returns to the beginning of that line to begin the next line.

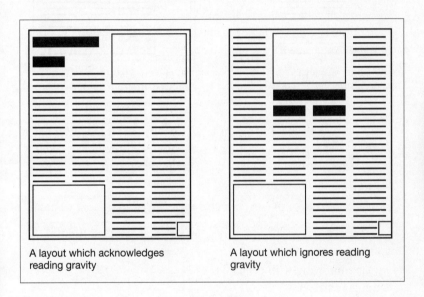

A layout which acknowledges reading gravity

A layout which ignores reading gravity

GIVING THE RIGHT IMPRESSION

The same principles apply to magazine layouts:

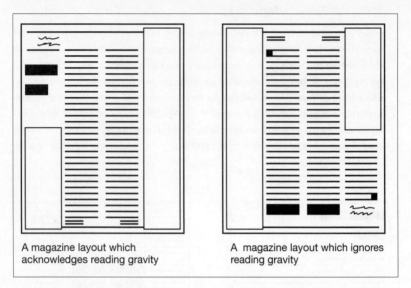

A magazine layout which
acknowledges reading gravity

A magazine layout which ignores
reading gravity

When it comes to measuring how well people comprehend what is written on these pages – in other words how well they have taken in your message – it becomes clear that you ignore gravity at your peril.

Layout	Comprehension level		
	Good	Fair	Poor
Layout complying with principles of reading gravity	67	19	14
Layout disregarding reading gravity	32	30	38

There's another element to layout as well, particularly when it comes to double page spreads. If your readers are opening up a spread in, say, a brochure or a magazine, there is a risk they won't even get as far as reading it. So you need to make the layout appeal to the eye sufficiently to persuade your targets to read the piece more fully.

Colin Wheildon's research refers to the studies carried out by Professor Siegfried Vogele, and says:

When a potential reader comes upon a spread, the eyes alight at the top right corner, possibly because this is the first point exposed when a leaflet is opened or a newspaper or magazine page turned. From this point at the top right corner the eyes make a parabolic sweep to the left and then back down to the right, sending messages to the brain when they make a fix on display elements. At the end of that sweep the brain makes a decision, based on the number or magnitude of the fixes made, whether there's enough incentive to read the spread.

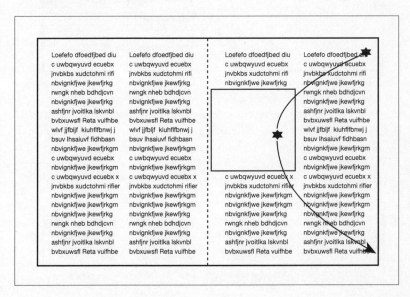

A good display, which attracts the eye with a headline, illustrations and so on, will extend the sweep towards those design elements.

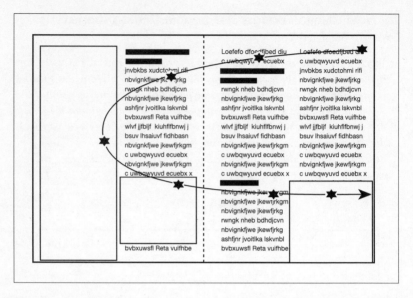

On the other hand, if there are few display elements, or none at all, the eye barely skims the right margin of the page and the potential reader is highly unlikely to decide to read the whole piece.

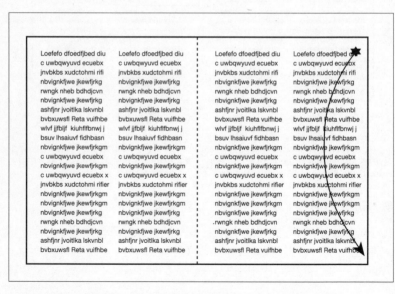

Source: *Communicating or Just Making Pretty Shapes*, Colin Wheildon, Newspaper Advertising Bureau of Australia Limited

■ *How can you encourage people to read the text?*

If you've got a lot to say, you're going to have to say at least some of it in chunks of body text (what some typographers call body type). The problem is that long stretches of text can look fairly uninviting. So what can you do to make it look more interesting or readable?

- 38% of readers found body type set wider than 60 characters hard to read.

- Another 22% indicated they probably wouldn't read wide measure body type even though they didn't find any difficulty reading it.

- 87% said they found extremely narrow measure, such as less than 20 characters, hard to read.

- 78% indicated they found cross headings useful, particularly in long articles. No one said they found cross headings unattractive or intrusive.

The following sections on legibility and colour also contain pointers to encourage people to read body type.

Source: Communicating or Just Making Pretty Shapes, Colin Wheildon, Newspaper Advertising Bureau of Australia Limited

■ *Which are best – photos or illustrations?*

There are times when you don't have a choice, of course, but assuming that you have an option, which will have the greater impact on your readers?

- Photographs were recalled far more clearly than drawings, by more than half of those who read the test leaflets.

Source: Communicating or Just Making Pretty Shapes, Colin Wheildon, Newspaper Advertising Bureau of Australia Limited

■ *Should you justify text?*

If you haven't come across this term before, it has nothing to do with offering excuses for what you have written! In justified text, the right hand ends of all the lines are lined up. If they are not, you have ragged right setting (assuming the left hand ends are still flush). If you line up the right ends but start the left hand ends in different places, you have ragged left setting.

The question is: does the type of setting you use affect your readers' comprehension levels?

Setting	Comprehension level		
	Good	Fair	Poor
Layout with totally justified setting	67	19	14
Layout with ragged right setting	38	22	40
Layout with ragged left setting	10	18	72

Source: Communicating or Just Making Pretty Shapes, Colin Wheildon, Newspaper Advertising Bureau of Australia Limited

Readability

■ *Do people find serif or sans serif type easier to read?*

Serifs, as you probably know, are the twiddly bits at the corners of letters in certain typefaces; a sans serif type has 'smooth' letters.

Serif type   Sans serif type

Aa Aa

So do these little twiddly bits really make any difference to how easy your text is to read and comprehend? Apparently they make a considerable difference. Some people actually find it physically uncomfortable to read sans serif type because of the eye tiredness it causes them. Others find it hard to focus or keep having to backtrack to recall points they have just read.

Type	Comprehension level		
	Good	Fair	Poor
Layout with serif body type	67	19	14
Layout with sans serif body type	12	23	65

Source: *Communicating or Just Making Pretty Shapes*, Colin Wheildon, Newspaper Advertising Bureau of Australia Limited

■ Do people find capitals or lower case letters more legible?

Nobody is advocating that you adopt e e cummings's approach of dropping initial capital letters. But when it comes to setting whole headlines or more in capitals, does this make a difference to readability? Apparently so. It seems that we largely recognise words by their shape, but if you use solid capitals every word is virtually the same shape: rectangular. For the purposes of this part of the research, respondents were shown a collection of headlines set in various type styles and asked 'Do you find this easy to read – yes or no?'

Headline style	Lower case	Capitals
Roman old style	92	69
Roman modern	89	71
Sans serif	90	57
Optima	85	56
Square serif	64	44

Bear in mind that this part of the research only considered capital letters in headlines, not in body text. However it's not unreasonable to assume that large chunks of body type set in capital letters would be the same only worse.

Source: *Communicating or Just Making Pretty Shapes*, Colin Wheildon, Newspaper Advertising Bureau of Australia Limited

■ *Is emboldened text easier or harder to read?*

Putting text in **bold** type certainly makes it stand out, but at what cost? Once you have drawn people's attention to it, you presumably want them to read it. But that's where you could hit problems with emboldened type. Some readers in these tests complained of fatigue after reading bold body text, while others found it created a halo effect where the outlines of the letters appeared to be carried into adjoining letters and the lines above and below.

Body text	Comprehension level		
	Good	Fair	Poor
Text printed in Times Roman	70	19	11
Text printed in Times Bold	30	20	50

These tests were conducted using emboldened body type, not single headings, subheadings and so on. There are no specific figures on this but emboldening single, short cross headings, for example, may gain you more in impact than it loses in readability.

Source: *Communicating or Just Making Pretty Shapes*, Colin Wheildon, Newspaper Advertising Bureau of Australia Limited

■ *Are italics harder to read?*

Many people who know a little bit about typography will tell you that italics are notoriously hard to read. But where are they getting their information from? Certainly there are some italic type faces that you would expect to be difficult to read since they also possess some other hard-to-read property – for example they may be emboldened, contain elaborate flourishes or be sans serif.

But, generally speaking, there is no reason why italic text should be hard to read, once people have got over their initial reaction to a chunk of text in an unusual type face. This is borne out by the research.

Body text	Comprehension level		
	Good	Fair	Poor
Layout using Corona Roman text	67	19	14
Layout using Corona Italic text	65	19	16

Source: *Communicating or Just Making Pretty Shapes*, Colin Wheildon, Newspaper Advertising Bureau of Australia Limited

■ *Which styles of headline type are easiest to read?*

Even when you're only using a type face for a few words, the difference in legibility can be enormous. This study tested twenty-four

The legibility scale		
1	Roman old style lower case	92
2	Sans serif lower case	90
3	Roman modern lower case	89
4	Roman old style italic lower case	86
5	Roman modern italic lower case	86
6	Sans serif italic lower case	86
7	Optima lower case	85
8	Optima italic lower case	80
9	Roman modern capitals	71
10	Roman old style capitals	69
11	Square serif lower case	64
12	Roman modern italic capitals	63
13	Roman old style italic capitals	62
14	Sans serif italic capitals	59
15	Optima italic capitals	57
16	Sans serif capitals	57
17	Optima capitals	56
18	Square serif capitals	44
19	Cursive or script lower case	37
20*	Ornamented lower case	24–32

21	Cursive or script capitals	26
22*	Ornamented capitals	11–19
23	Black letter lower case	10
24	Black letter capitals	3

*The ornamented faces come in various forms, and a range of responses is given

different headline styles and found a range of scores between 92 and 3 out of 100 on the legibility scale.

Source: *Communicating or Just Making Pretty Shapes*, Colin Wheildon, Newspaper Advertising Bureau of Australia Limited

■ Which type sizes are easiest to read as continuous text?

Clearly you're not going to print your body text so small that you have to supply a free magnifying glass with every copy; nor do you want each paragraph to occupy an entire page. But even within a sensible-sounding range of type sizes, there can be a surprising range of legibility. In the tests, respondents were asked to identify which of several type sizes they found easy to read. The table that follows also shows what type size on what body size was most commonly considered easy to read. (The body size is the space between the bottom of one line and the bottom of the next; so 10 point type on 12 point body – 10/12 – would give 2 points of space between the top of one upstroke and the bottom of the downstroke above it.)

Type size	'easy to read' percentage	Type size	'easy to read' percentage
8 point	14	12	72
8/9	21	12/13	90
8/10	26	12/14	82
9	63	13	66
9/10	66	13/14	70
9/11	71	13/15	68
10	69	14	59
10/11	86	14/15	61
10/12	92	14/16	63
11	77	15	21
11/12	93	15/16	25
11/13	98	15/17	28

Source: Communicating or Just Making Pretty Shapes, Colin Wheildon, Newspaper Advertising Bureau of Australia Limited

■ *Does kerning affect legibility (and what is it, anyway)?*

No, it's not a knitting instruction (purl two, kern three). You can squeeze letters closer together without changing their shape; for example you can edge a capital A up closer to a W. This is kerning. You can kern in units, from one to three, or even four. You or your designer might think it looks prettier, or that it means you can fit the headline all on one line without having to reduce the point size. But while you may get away with kerning one unit, you should think twice before you go any further. The following tables indicate the positive response as a percentage of the total sample.

Times Roman:			
Lower case		**Capitals**	
natural	93	natural	68
kerned one unit	92	kerned one unit	66
two units	67	two units	53
three units	44	three units	41
four units	0	four units	0

Helvetica Bold:			
Lower case		**Capitals**	
natural	92	natural	55
kerned one unit	93	kerned one unit	56
two units	79	two units	48
three units	74	three units	44
four units	0	four units	0

Source: Communicating or Just Making Pretty Shapes, Colin Wheildon, Newspaper Advertising Bureau of Australia Limited

■ *How legible is 'reversed out' text?*

If you print in a light colour type on a dark background – usually done as white on black – this is known as reversed out text. Some people maintain that it is worth using as it attracts the reader's attention, but the results of this study suggest that even if this is true, it still isn't worth it.

Reversed or not?	Comprehension level		
	Good	Fair	Poor
Text printed black on white	70	19	11
Text printed white on black	0	12	88

Source: Communicating or Just Making Pretty Shapes, Colin Wheildon, Newspaper Advertising Bureau of Australia Limited

■ How easy is it to read black text on a grey background?

Suppose you want to call attention to a section of text by printing it on a grey background? You can vary the shade of grey you use from, say, 10% of black, which is very light grey, upwards (100% is black).

Background	Comprehension level		
	Good	Fair	Poor
Black on white	70	19	11
Black on 10% black	63	22	15
Black on 20% black	33	18	49
Black on 30% black	3	10	87

Source: Communicating or Just Making Pretty Shapes, Colin Wheildon, Newspaper Advertising Bureau of Australia Limited

■ Do people find it easier to read from matt or gloss paper?

Have you ever wondered whether your target readers find it harder to read from gloss paper because of reflections?

● The tests for this research were initially conducted separately on matt and gloss paper. However, when tests failed to show any significant variation in comprehension levels, they eventually abandoned this distinction and continued using matt paper only.

Source: Communicating or Just Making Pretty Shapes, Colin Wheildon, Newspaper Advertising Bureau of Australia Limited

Colour

■ *Are your targets more likely to read and understand headlines in coloured type?*

There's an argument that coloured headlines attract the reader's attention more than those printed in black. But how easy are they to read? Of course, it depends partly on what colour you use. The study tested both high chroma colours (such as cyan and magenta) and low chroma colours (such as dark emerald and plum red).

- 61% of all readers said they found the high chroma colours most attractive, drawing their attention quickly to the text.

- But 47% said they then found the high chroma headings hard to read.

- 12% said the high chroma colours had the same effect as an obtrusive light, distracting the eyes.

- 10% found the high chroma colours intense and tending to cause eye-tiredness.

Headlines	Comprehension level		
	Good	Fair	Poor
Layout with black headlines	67	19	14
Layout using high chroma colour headlines	17	18	65
Layout using low chroma colour headlines	52	28	20

The results seem to suggest that while brighter colours attract the reader, the brighter they are, the harder they are to read.

Source: Communicating or Just Making Pretty Shapes, Colin Wheildon, Newspaper Advertising Bureau of Australia Limited

■ *How easy is it to read text on a tinted background?*

We've already established that black on anything but the palest of greys is not a good idea. But what about black on a tint of a colour? After all, it should attract attention, so is it worth it? The tests were carried out using black on tints of cyan (primary blue).

Background	Comprehension level		
	Good	Fair	Poor
Black on 10% cyan	68	24	8
Black on 20% cyan	56	21	23
Black on 30% cyan	38	19	43
Black on 40% cyan	22	12	66

Source: Communicating or Just Making Pretty Shapes, Colin Wheildon, Newspaper Advertising Bureau of Australia Limited

■ *How will your readers respond to coloured text?*

If coloured headlines attract more attention, but then become distracting, could you use a black headline but attract the reader with coloured text?

● The tests used five different colours of text (including black) on white paper. 90% of the sample said they thought the black page looked boring compared with the blue printed page.

● 81% said they would prefer to read the coloured page because it was more attractive.

● However, 76% of the sample said they found text printed in high intensity colours difficult to read.

● 63% said the medium intensity colour provided concentration problems.

● Every one of the readers said they would prefer to read text printed in black.

GIVING THE
RIGHT IMPRESSION

Text colour	Comprehension level		
	Good	Fair	Poor
Text printed in black	70	19	11
Low intensity colour (deep purple)	51	13	36
Medium intensity colour (French blue)	29	22	49
Muted colour (olive green)	10	13	77
High intensity colour (cyan or warm red)	10	9	81

Source: Communicating or Just Making Pretty Shapes, Colin Wheildon, Newspaper Advertising Bureau of Australia Limited

■ *Is it worth paying for spot colour in an ad?*

Just because coloured headlines and text are harder to read, it doesn't mean you can't use any spot colour at all. Just keep it away from the words. But its value in attracting attention is not to be sniffed at, especially when it comes to advertising.

● According to one piece of research, spot colour generally adds to the cost of an ad by 20% or more, but the ad is noticed by 63% more people and results in 64% more sales.

Source: Communicating or Just Making Pretty Shapes, Colin Wheildon, Newspaper Advertising Bureau of Australia Limited

Language

■ *How can you be sure that your writing style is clear?*

Despite being taught basic writing skills at school, many people find it hard at times to keep their language clear and simple. We were unable to track down any quantified research into writing skills (except for data about levels of basic literacy, which are included in *The Essential Personnel Sourcebook*). However, you might find the following information helpful. It has been supplied by the Plain English Campaign, who have spent over 20 years helping people write clearly and, during that time, have built up an invaluable body of wisdom on the key guidelines for writing material that is easy to understand.

When you write...

Put yourself in the reader's shoes and use:

- Short sentences; average 15–20 words a sentence
- Everyday words wherever possible, and explain any technical terms you have to use
- 'You' and 'we' instead of 'the customer', 'the company' and so on
- Active verbs, rather than passive verbs. In other words, write 'We will pay this into your account when we get your letter telling us...' rather than 'Payment will be made when your letter is received'
- Plenty of 'signposts' to help your reader find what they are looking for. These include headings and sub-headings, contents lists (for documents such as sales proposals), and lists of key features (like this one).

Source: Plain English Campaign

Appendix 1
HOW TO READ STATISTICS

This book is packed with statistical figures – percentages, average marks out of ten, tables, graphs, charts. After a while it can become hard to take in so much information in this form. There are also various conventions and standard formulas that are used to analyse and present such statistics. It seemed worthwhile to give brief descriptions and explanations of these in case you haven't come across them before, or not for a long time, and might benefit from some clarification of what it all actually means.

This appendix, then, is intended to clarify some of the types of statistical data that can be found in *The Essential Personnel Sourcebook,* and *The Essential Marketing Sourcebook.* Of course, it may come in handy any time that you are presented with some statistics and would like to refresh your memory of what exactly they are telling you, or not telling you. It is also intended to clear up some of the confusions that can easily be caused by the use of technical terms, particular formats and so on.

CHARTS, GRAPHS AND MATRICES

There are many charts included in this book, and each has been picked to present the data in the most convenient way. It is therefore worth mentioning the particular properties and uses of each chart, so that you will know at a glance what is being presented. The easiest way to do this is to go through the different types of chart and give a brief explanation of each one.

Bar chart

This is one of the most common types of chart. It shows figures (usually quantity or percentage) for various different items. For example, it might show what percentage of people in an office have each of the following items of fruit in their fruit bowl at home:

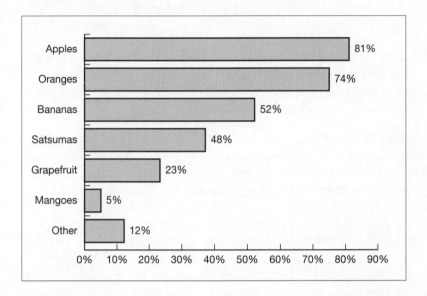

As with this chart, the highest number (and hence longest bar) should come at the top, with the others decreasing in order. Certain categories are exceptions to this rule, by always coming at the end. The most common of these are 'other' and 'none' (which may occur, for instance, in a survey of what the people in the office had for breakfast). The figures in this example do not add up to 100%, of course, since many people have more than one type of fruit in their fruit bowl.

Column chart

This looks very similar to a bar chart, but the blocks go up rather than across. Despite this similarity, it is used in a significantly different way from a bar chart. It is used in instances where the different columns progress along a sequence. Typical examples of this are when the figures apply to different times (1990, 1991, 1992, etc.), different scores (strongly agree, agree, not sure, disagree, strongly disagree), and different age groups (16–19, 20–23, 24–35, 36–39). This last example is important since the groupings given are not equal. The column for people age 24–35 is likely to be much larger than for the other groupings, since it covers a much wider range of people. This sort of distortion is worth looking out for in general (although in this series we have avoided it wherever possible), and has a certain amount of effect every time there is an open-ended group (e.g. age 40+).

Since the different categories in a column chart follow a sequence, the relative heights become much more important. For instance, let's see a graph of the number of people in the office with apples in their fruit bowls for each of the last 4 weeks.

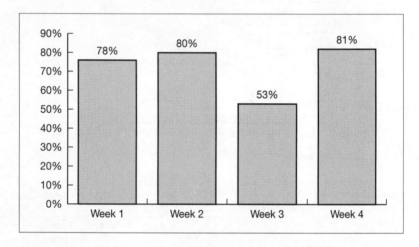

Perhaps there was a major deadline at work at the end of Week 3 and no one had time to go shopping. It is variations like this that are the main point of information in most Column Charts.

Pie chart

A pie chart is used in similar cases to a bar chart, but there is one special property of a pie chart. This is that the figures in it *must* add up to 100%. Of course, the figures may be given as quantities rather than percentages, but there are no overlaps or omissions – the total sample is divided up completely between the various sections of the chart. For example, let's look at one fruit bowl, and see how many pieces of each type of fruit there are in it:

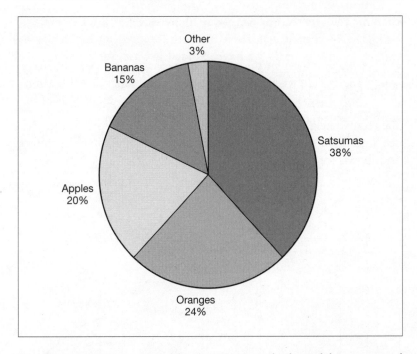

The largest segment should start at 12 o'clock and be measured clockwise from there, with subsequent segments being progressively smaller. In this way, the chart not only shows which figure is largest, but also visually conveys the relative sizes of the sections very effectively. Of course, it can be confusing if you try to fit 18 segments into a pie chart, so these are generally only used when there are 6 sections or fewer. Also, since the main strength of a pie chart is to convey relative sizes, there may be times when a bar chart is used instead, since this is not the main significance of the figures.

Line graph

These are used almost exclusively to show changes over time, and also sometimes to show changes according to age group. As we have seen, column charts can also be used for this purpose. The main differences between these two charts are:

- Column charts are only useful when there are relatively few figures – otherwise you end up with too many columns and it is hard to read.

- Column charts tend to be used to show specific variations rather than general trends.

So a line graph is used for time-series comparisons when there are many figures, and usually when there is a general trend rather than a horizontal line with a few kinks in it. An example would be an analysis of the number of apples I have eaten each week for the last 3 months.

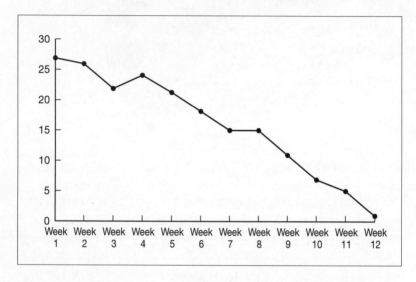

I am now completely sick of apples. What this chart conveys most effectively is the rapid decline in my apple addiction, rather than the number of apples that I ate in any given week.

Scatter chart

Scatter charts are used to show correlation – that is, the relationship between two factors. In this way, they could be used to show the relationship between the value of the pound and my tendency to eat apples. There is unlikely to be any real relationship here – both of these factors will vary without having any effect on each other. However, the relationship between the number of apples I eat and the number of bananas I eat may be very strong.

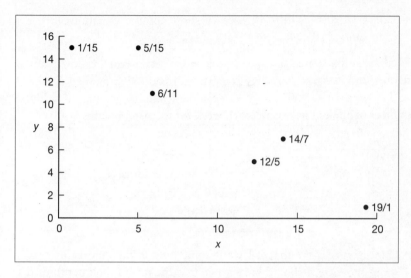

This shows that as my consumption of apples decreased (as shown by the values on the vertical Y-axis) my consumption of bananas increased (as shown by the value on the horizontal X-axis). So when I eat 15 apples, I eat one banana; when I eat one apple I eat 19 bananas. This can be seen from the fact that the points on the graph go in something approximating to a straight line from the top left to bottom right of the chart. If there were no correlation then they would not form any noticeable line. Scatter charts are quite uncommon, but are the most appropriate chart for showing this sort of correlation.

Matrix

Matrices vary from the other charts described here in that they are not necessarily dependent on numerical figures. The axes are normally shown crossed, giving a dead centre at the point where they cross. This divides the chart into four quarters, and the main information given is which quarter each item is in. In some matrices, items are not positioned any more specifically than this, while in others they are given a precise place on the chart.

Suppose, for instance, that I generally eat fruit either because it tastes nice, or because it is filling, and I want to know how well each type of fruit fills each of these criteria. If I were only interested in taste then I might give marks out of ten and show the results on a bar chart, but I want a chart that will show me both figures at once. The chart I want is this one:

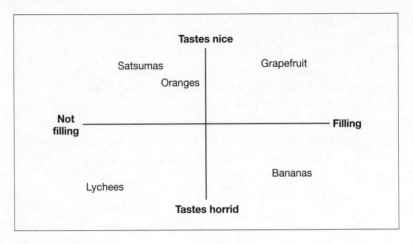

This chart tells me that if I want something filling, and I don't care about the taste, I should have a banana (the most filling item), or if I want it to taste nice as well, then I should have a grapefruit (not as filling, but much nicer). It also tells everyone exactly what I think of lychees. I could have given marks out of ten on each axis, which would have given each fruit a precise point on the graph, or I could have simply put each fruit in one of the four quarters and not been any more specific than this. The matrix above is a compromise between the two.

So matrices are useful for showing how a variety of items rate according to two different variables (e.g. taste and fillingness).

INDEXING

One particular statistical convention that may be used occasionally in these books is indexing. This is a relatively uncommon way of quantifying information, so it is probably worth giving a brief explanation of it for anyone who may not have come across it before.

Indexing is used when there are no absolute figures, only relative ones. The information therefore shows the relationships between these figures. However, this cannot be done with percentages or quantities. So how can the information be presented? The solution is to take an arbitrary figure as the standard, or as the maximum, and then rate other figures relative to this.

Suppose I want to rate how much Alice, Bruce, Cynthia and David enjoy eating apples. I am not asking for scores out of ten from each of them, I am trying to measure their actual enjoyment, so there is no absolute measurement that I can apply. However, I may still have meaningful and useful information to give on this topic. One way that I can present this is to say that Cynthia seems to be fairly ambivalent about eating apples, while the others have stronger feelings one way or the other. So I take 100 as the amount of pleasure Cynthia experiences from eating an apple. Using this, I now have a scale on which to judge the pleasure of my four subjects.

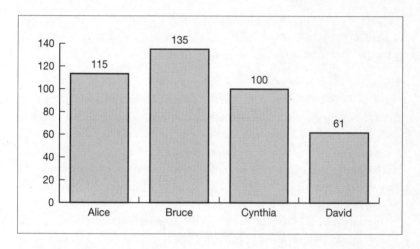

Note that the '100' here does not measure anything specific such as the volume of 'Mmmm' noises or number of endorphins released in the brain. And rather than having 100 as the most neutral point, I could have had it as the maximum enjoyment. This choice was entirely arbitrary, it was simply necessary to provide a way of presenting the data, and the data itself shows only the relationship between these four people's enjoyment of eating apples, and cannot be related to anything beyond this.

AVERAGES

Most of us can remember from school that there are three different kinds of average, even if we can't quite recall what all of them are. Since they are used in these books, it might be wise to recap them.

Imagine that 35 of us have fruit bowls, and I want to know the average number of apples in each bowl. My three options are:

1 Mean average: the total number of apples divided by the total number of fruit bowls (this is the most commonly used type of average, and the one that we generally mean when we don't specify which sort of average we are talking about).
2 Median average: the half way point between the highest (9) and lowest (0) number of apples.
3 Mode average: the single number of apples that occurs more frequently than any other.

I'll give you an example. The following line chart shows the number of fruit bowls containing each quantity of apples; 5 bowls have no apples in them, one contains one apple and so on.

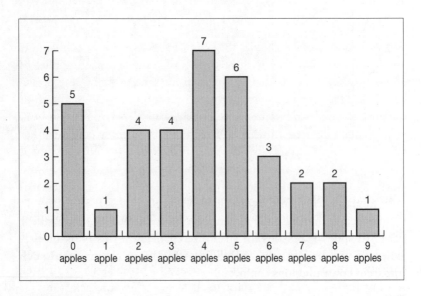

- Mean average number of apples (136 apples divided by 35 fruit bowls): 3.9
- Median average number of apples: 4.5
- Mode average number of apples: 7

FIGURES THAT SEEM TO CONTRADICT EACH OTHER

In books like *The Essential Personnel Sourcebook, The Essential Management and Finance Sourcebook* and *The Essential Marketing Sourcebook*, there are many figures which refer to very similar things. In some cases these figures may appear directly to contradict each other. In fact, we have taken great pains to ensure that no contradictory figures are included in any of *The Essential Business Sourcebooks*, but there are often subtle differences between statistics which are easy to overlook, and may give the impression that they cannot both be correct.

For example, suppose we are examining the composition of a particular fruit bowl which contains four satsumas and a grapefruit. We may say that:

● The contents of the fruit bowl are made up of 20% grapefruit.

● They are also made up of 50% grapefruit.

For the sake of this example, these figures are obviously deliberately unhelpful, but they may both be correct. The first, in fact, applies to the composition in numbers of fruits (four satsumas and one grapefruit), and the second applies to the composition in weight (since four satsumas weigh the same as one grapefruit). Naturally, we will explain such differences whenever there are potentially confusing figures like this in any of *The Essential Business Sourcebooks*, but if you are only looking up one piece of information, or if you are in a hurry and concentrating more on the figures than the text, then it is easy to miss such slight but crucial differences.

In order to minimise the likelihood of this happening, and make it easier to spot the reasons for such discrepancies in this book or elsewhere, I will briefly explains some of the main reasons that such apparent contradictions can occur.

Differences in the sample

Even if two surveys ask exactly the same question, it is exceptionally unlikely that they will be asking the same people. For this reason, results will always vary slightly between different surveys. Often surveys will deliberately be asking different people about the same thing – one survey may ask all workers, for instance, and another may be asking only managers. This may produce substantially different results, and these differences may even be the main point of interest in the figures.

The differences are sometimes even more subtle than this; for instance one survey may ask workplaces if they operate a certain policy, and another may ask workers if their workplace operates the policy. If the policy is most often operated by large workplaces with many employees, then the proportion of workers answering 'yes' is likely to be higher than the proportion of workplaces answering 'yes'.

Differences in survey characteristics

Sometimes differences may be less deliberate. One survey may have covered more large companies than another, for instance, and in many cases this will lead to different results. This does not mean that one was a survey of large companies and the other a survey of small companies, it simply means that their balance of companies of different sizes was not the same. Similarly, one survey may have been conducted by interview and another by postal questionnaire, and this will also have an effect on the results.

Another factor that may lead to differences is the time of the survey. Figures of change over time can be very useful information in its own right, but since any two surveys are likely to vary in many ways (such as what exact question was asked, who was asked and so on) it is often misleading to compare results from two totally different surveys conducted at different times.

To avoid this type of confusion, the figures in this book have been selected as the most reliable ones of all that were available. However, there may be times when two different surveys cover the same topic but ask slightly different questions, in which cases both will be included, in order to provide as much useful information as possible. In such cases, it is worth remembering that the two surveys were very probably conducted at different times and in different ways, and while both are informative and valid, they are unlikely to have produced exactly the same results.

Differences in conceptual structure

Many decisions are made when designing a survey, and this is another area where surveys can vary. If I am conducting a survey into how many people eat apples often, then I will have to define 'often'. Is it once a week, twice a week, or once a fortnight? Naturally, the choice I make in defining this term will affect what figure I arrive at the end of the survey.

Similarly, I may be surveying how many apples people eat in a week. If I am doing this on a tick-box questionnaire, then I will have to choose what categories to provide a box for – it may be '0–3', '4–8', '8–11', '12+', or it may be '0', '1–5', '6–10', '11+'. It will be very hard to tie together the two sets of figures that I receive, and each grouping has its own strengths and weaknesses.

Similarly, I may be surveying people's favourite fruits, and listing them either by colour, or by price, or in groups such as citrus, tropical and so on. Again, I may not be able to compare the different results that I receive in any meaningful way. Each set of results will tell me something that I want to know, but will fail to tell me something else. So each set of results simply has to be taken on its own merits, and the inherent differences borne in mind when taking the results together.

NOT ADDING UP TO 100%

In this book, and elsewhere, percentage figures are often given which do not total 100%. At times this may be confusing, particularly when you want to be sure that you have complete and reliable information. Of course, there are many legitimate reasons why this can occur, and it is worth running through these quickly so that, when such a situation occurs, you will be able to see why it has happened.

More than 100%

Rounding

Some of the figures that are given as whole number percentages may originally have been calculated to one or two decimal places. This level of detail is often unnecessary, and can complicate the information that is being given, and hence the figures have been 'rounded' to the nearest whole number. This process can occasionally produce figures which total 101% or 102%, although it is rare to create any more of a disturbance than this.

For example, the composition of my fruit bowl (by weight) is:

Apples:	30.6%
Oranges:	32.7%
Bananas:	36.6%

This makes a total of 100%. However, I would like to make these statistics easier to read and take in, so I want them as whole numbers. Since the numbers after the decimal places are all greater than 5, this means that all these numbers will be rounded up, giving this composition:

Apples: 31%
Oranges: 33%
Bananas: 37%

This totals 101%. This is an unfortunate, but unavoidable, effect of rounding. Although it can be disconcerting, the only way to treat it is simply to accept that it happens, but that it causes only very minimal distortion of the statistics, since the total of the percentages very rarely comes to more than 102%.

Multiple answers

Let's consider the example given earlier in this section of the proportion of people with each given fruit in their fruit bowl:

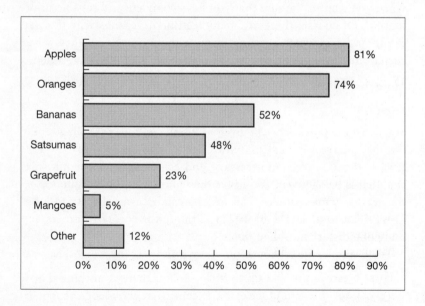

The total here is obviously much greater than 100%. The simple reason for this is that many people have more than one fruit in their bowl. Questions like this, for which each individual can give more than one answer, often end up with figures that total more than 100%. So long as we do not find that 117% of people have apples in their fruit bowl, then the data is perfectly correct.

Overlapping categories

I have found that my fruit bowl contains (by quantity), 50% tropical fruit and 70% citrus fruit. These figures seem hard to reconcile, but of course there is an explanation for this. This explanation involves grapefruit, which I class as a citrus fruit and also as a tropical fruit. My fruit bowl contains 5 satsumas, 3 bananas and 2 grapefruit. Hence there are 7 citrus fruits (satsumas and grapefruit) and 5 tropical fruits (bananas and grapefruit).

It is often useful to collect information in groupings which do not have overlaps, so as to provide a total figure of 100%. However, it may also be that two particular groups are of interest (e.g. tropical and citrus fruits), and that these groups have an overlap. If so, the figures for these groups, when added together, may total more than 100%.

Less than 100%

Rounding

The effects of rounding, as discussed previously, can produce figures which total less than 100%. On re-examining my fruit bowl, I have discovered its composition (by weight) to be:

Apples:	31.3%
Oranges:	32.4%
Bananas:	36.3%

This, again, totals 100%. After rounding, however, the figures are:

Apples:	31%
Oranges:	32%
Bananas:	36%

These figures only add up to 99%. Again, there is nothing that I can do about this rounding error, except to acknowledge that it is unavoidable, and causes only minimal distortion of the statistics.

Omitted categories

The most obvious categories which could be relevant here are 'Not Answered' and 'Don't Know'. If I ask everyone in my office whether they have apples in their fruit bowl at home, I may find that

- 72% do have apples;
- Only 25% do not have apples.

But what about the other 3%? Well, maybe they didn't know, or maybe they just didn't want to say. Maybe they all, in fact, do have apples at home, and maybe none of them do. We simply can't say, and we have to ignore them.

Sometimes figures for D/K or N/A are given, showing how many people did not respond to the question, and at other times they are not. Many survey questions, however, do not receive a full quota of answers, but the number not responding is usually fairly low and, as with rounding, does not undermine the other data to any appreciable extent.

Of course, other categories can be omitted when data is presented – any category can. If I ask my workmates what their favourite fruit is, I may find that:

- Apples are favourite for 43%.
- Bananas are the next most popular, cited by 31%.
- Oranges are preferred by only 14%.
- 4% did not know or did not answer.

This gives a total of 92%. So what about the other 8%? Well, some of them preferred mangoes, others went for satsumas or guava – there were various answers. However, the proportion who opted for each was so low that it did not seem worth including them. The information that I was trying to convey was how popular the most popular fruits are, not a full breakdown with details of fruits that were favourite with only 0.3% of people.

Although *The Essential Business Sourcebooks* try to be as comprehensive as possible, they are designed for practical use, and hence some figures may have been omitted in this way when they were not significant or relevant, and would serve only to confuse the data provided. Such detail may also have been omitted in the source literature from which the statistics were gathered. For these reasons, categories may sometimes have been omitted, giving figures that add up to less than 100%. In these cases, the data is indeed not comprehensive, but the figures that are given are no less valid for it.

Appendix 2
CONTACT ADDRESSES OF
CONTRIBUTING ORGANISATIONS

ACAS
The Advisory, Conciliation and Arbitration Service,
Brandon House, 180 Borough High Street, London, SE1 1LW
0171 210 3613, fax 0171 210 3645

The Advertising Association
Abford House, 15 Wilton Road, London, SW1V 1NJ
0171 828 2771, fax 0171 931 0376
Email: Advert@dial.pipex.com

The Aziz Corporation
West Stratton, Winchester, Hampshire, SO21 3DR
01962 776766

Barclays Bank plc Small Business Services
54, Lombard Street, London, EC3P 3AH

The Basic Skills Agency
Commonwealth House, 1–19 New Oxford Street, London, WC1A 1NU
0171 405 4071

Bemrose UK Ltd
Waygoose Drive, PO Box 82, Derby DE21 6XL
01332 294242

The Drayton Bird Partnership
MCB House, 133–137 Westbourne Grove, London, W11 2RS
0171 243 0196, fax 0171 229 0426
Email: 101476.252@compuserve.com

British Chambers of Commerce
BCC Publications, Manning House, 22 Carlisle Place, London, SW1P 1JA
0171 565 2033, fax 0171 565 2049
Email: 100563.415@compuserve.com

British Telecom
BT Telemarketing Services
0800 66 00 99

Calcom Group Ltd
Heston Court, Camp Road, Wimbledon, London, SW19 4UW
0181 944 9669, fax 0181 944 9779
Email: telebusiness@calcom.co.uk

Chartered Institute of Marketing
Marketing Department, Moor Hall, Cookham,
Maidenhead, Berkshire, SL6 9QH
01628 427500, fax 01628 427499
http://www.cim.co.uk

Chartered Institute of Purchasing and Supply
Easton House, Easton-on-the-Hill, Stamford, Lincolnshire, PE9 3NZ
01780 756777, fax 01780 751610
Email: info@cips.org
http://www.cips.org

Citizen's Charter Unit
Horse Guards Road, London, SW1P 3AL
0171 270 0302, fax 0171 270 6327
Email: charter@gtnet.gov.uk
http://www.open.gov.uk/charter/ccuhome.htm

The Direct Mail Information Service
5, Carlisle Street, London, W1V 5RG
0171 494 0483, fax 0171 494 0455
http://www.dmis.co.uk

The Direct Marketing Association
Haymarket House, 1 Oxenden Street, London, SW1Y 4EE
0171 321 2525, fax 0171 321 0191

The Dryden Press
24–28 Oval Road, London, NW1 7DX
0171 267 4466, fax 0171 485 1140
Email:jennifer@dryden.hbuk.co.uk

ESOMAR
JJ Viottastraat 29, 1071 JP Amsterdam, The Netherlands
+31 20 664 2141, fax +31 20 664 2922

Exhibition Industry Federation
115 Hartington Road, London, SW8 2HB
0171 498 3306, fax 0171 627 8287
Email: hn23@dial.pipex.com

John Fenton Training International plc
Clifford Hill Court, Clifford Chambers, Stratford-upon-Avon, CV37 8AA
01789 298739, fax 01789 267060

Hallmark Public Relations
Canister House, 27 Jewry Street, London, SW8 2HB
01962 863850, fax 01962 841820
Email: 100540.101@compuserve.com

Henley Centre for Forecasting
Marketing Department, 9, Bridewell Place, Blackfriars, London, EC4V 6AY
0171 353 9961, fax 0171 353 2899

Hewson Consulting Group
Barclay House, 13 High Street, Olney, Buckinghamshire, MK46 4EB
01234 713351, fax 01234 241586

The Institute of Direct Marketing
No 1 Park Road, Teddington, Middlesex, TW11 0AR
0181 977 5705, fax 0181 943 2535

Institute of Logisitics
Douglas House, Queens Square, Corby, Northamptonshire, NN17 1PL
01536 205500, fax 01536 400979

Institute of Management Foundation
Management House, Cottingham Road, Corby,
Northamptonshire, NN17 1TT
01536 204222, fax 01536 201651

The L & R Group
70, South Lambert Road, London, SW8 1RL
0171 735 4000

MCB University Press (*European Journal of Marketing*)
62 Toller Lane, Bradford, West Yorkshire, BD8 9BY
01274 777700, fax 01274 785200

McGraw-Hill Book Company Europe
Shoppenhangers Road, Maidenhead, Berkshire, SL6 2QL
01628 23432

Managing the Service Business
Winslow House, Church Lane, Sunninghill, Ascot, Berkshire, SL5 7ED
01344 876300, fax 01344 873677

National Consumer Council
20 Grosvenor Gardens, London, SW1W 0DH
0171 730 3469, fax 0171 730 0191

National Dairy Council
5–7 Princes Street, London, W1M 0AP
0171 499 7822

NatWest UK
Small Business Services, Level 10 Drapers Gardens,
12 Throgmorton Avenue, London, EC4A 1PR
0171 920 5555
Email: peter.stern@natwestuk.co.uk

To order the *NatWest/BFA Franchise survey*, contact:
British Franchise Association, Thames View, Newtown Road
Henley-on-Thames, Oxfordshire, RG9 1HG
01491 575903, fax 01491 573517

Newspaper Advertising Bureau of Australia
PO Box 314, Milsons Point, 2061 New South Wales, Australia
+61 2 955 8599

Office of Fair Trading
Room 306, Field House, Bream's Buildings, London, EC4V 1PR
0171 211 8000, fax 0171 211 8800
Email: enquiries@oftuk.demon.co.uk

P-E International
Logistics Services
Park House, Wick Road, Egham, Surrey, TW20 0HW
01784 434411, fax 01784 476403

Plain English Campaign
PO Box 3, New Mills, Stockport, Cheshire, SK12 4QP
01663 744409

The Policy Studies Institute
100 Park Village East, London, NW1 3SR
0171 468 0468

Radio Advertising Bureau
74 Newman Street, London, W1P 3LA
0171 636 5858

RAJAR
Collier House, 163–169 Brompton Road, London, SW3 1PY
0171 584 3003, fax 0171 589 4004

Regester Larkin Ltd
505 Coppergate House, 16 Brune Street, London, E1 7NJ
0171 721 7395, fax 0171 721 7810

The Research Business
Holford Mews, Cruickshank Street, London, WC1X 9HD
0171 837 1242

Research Services Ltd
Research Services House, Elm Grove Road, Harrow, Middlesex, HA1 2QG
0181 861 6000

Richmond Events Ltd
London House, 243–253 Lower Mortlake Road,
Richmond, Surrey, TW9 2LS
0181 322 2422

Small Business Research Trust
University of Westminster, 35 Marylebone Road, London, NW1 5LS
0171 911 5000

Strathmoor Press
2550 Ninth Street, Suite 1040, Berkeley, California, USA
+1 510 843 8888, fax +1 510 843 0142

The Survey Shop
20 Reabrook Avenue, Shrewsbury, Shropshire, SY3 7QA
01743 352041, fax 01743 241941

TARP Europe Ltd
6 Spring Gardens, Citadel Place, Tinworth Street, London, SE11 5EH
0171 793 1866, fax 0171 793 1940

VA Research
7 Chiswick High Road, London, W4 2ND
0181 994 9177, fax 0181 994 2115

Welbeck Golin/Harris Communications Ltd
43 King Street, Covent Garden, London, WC2E 8RJ
0171 836 6677, fax 0171 836 5820